Americans Behind the Iron Curtain

Americans Behind the Iron Curtain

Tales of Detention, Resilience, and Freedom in Cold War East Berlin

Sabina Wiedenhoeft Dugan

Washington, DC

New Academia Publishing/VELLUM Books, 2024

Printed in the United States of America

Library of Congress Control Number: 2024907322
ISBN 979-8-9875893-9-7 paperback (alk. paper)

 An imprint of New Academia Publishing

 New Academia Publishing
4401-A Connecticut Ave. NW, #236, Washington DC 20008
info@newacademia.com - www.newacademia.com

Contents

Two thousand years ago the proudest boast was civis romanus sum *[I am a citizen of Rome]. Today, in the world of freedom, the proudest boast is 'Ich bin ein Berliner!' … Freedom is indivisible, and when one man is enslaved, all are not free… All free men, wherever they may live, are citizens of Berlin, and therefore, as a free man, I take pride in the words, Ich bin ein Berliner.* (President John F. Kennedy in West Berlin, 26 June 1963)

Preface
History of the Divided Berlin

This story takes place in Berlin during the 1960s when the city was divided by the Wall and West Berlin was an island of freedom and prosperity surrounded by Communist East Germany. The divided city was emblematic of the Cold War tensions that existed between East and West and routinely witnessed confrontations between the world's largest superpowers — the United States and the Soviet Union.

In the United States, anxious Americans followed escalating Cold War tensions by tuning into news reports broadcast on the television and radio and reading newspapers. Real-time reporting of events from around the world had recently become possible with direct transmission to the broadcast networks. The 1960s became the decade of television news, starting with the presidential debate between John F. Kennedy and Richard Nixon in 1960, the 1962 Cuban Missile Crisis, the 1963 assassination of President Kennedy and the ongoing war footage from Vietnam.

Where television brought news headlines into a growing number of homes, newspapers still offered more in-depth coverage and interpretation of events. In their quest for stories, newspapers and broadcasters relied upon news organizations such as the Associated Press (AP), United Press International (UPI) and the British-based Reuters for on-site reporting and images. These press agencies transmitted news material to thousands of newspapers, magazines, radio, and television stations in the United States and abroad. Reuters, for example, scooped the news of the construction of the Berlin Wall in 1961.

When seven Americans, including my own father Ronald Wiedenhoeft, a graduate student at Columbia University, were imprisoned in East Germany during the second half of the 1960s, AP, UPI and Reuters delivered detailed reports on their arrest, sentencing and eventual release. These newswire dispatches were transmitted and published in newspapers all over the United States and Germany, as well as other nations. Local, regional, and national publications such as *The New York Times*, *The Washington Post*, *The Chicago Tribune*, *The International Herald Tribune*, *Die Welt*, *Frankfurter Allgemeine Zeitung*, *Berliner Morgenpost*, and many others featured articles on the prisoners' predicament.

Readers' interest in these events was piqued not only for its human-interest component, but as confirmation of the threat of communism. If idealistic young men and women could be arrested and subjected to psychological terror for what was perceived as harmless misdemeanors or trumped-up charges, what was the world coming to? How could a doctoral student be branded a spy for gathering material for his dissertation? These stories highlighted the idealistic disparities between the freedom-loving West and the paranoid mentality behind the Iron Curtain. From Western perspective, the clash between democracy and communism became personified in the plight of these American prisoners.

Only diplomatic finesse could untangle this cultural impasse. The improbable involvement of the American lawyer Maxwell Rabb, who had a special gift for communicating, a belief in the goodness of people and high-ranking government connections, bridged this cultural divide and opened new channels of negotiation and trade between East and West.

History of the Divided Berlin

After World War II, the fate of Berlin was decided at the Yalta Conference of February 1945 and the Potsdamer Conference of August 1945. The city, like the rest of Germany, was divided into four German occupied zones — American, British, French, and Soviets. The Allies wanted to denazify and demilitarize Germany, working towards eventual reconstruction and formation of a peaceful democracy. While the American, British and French Allies

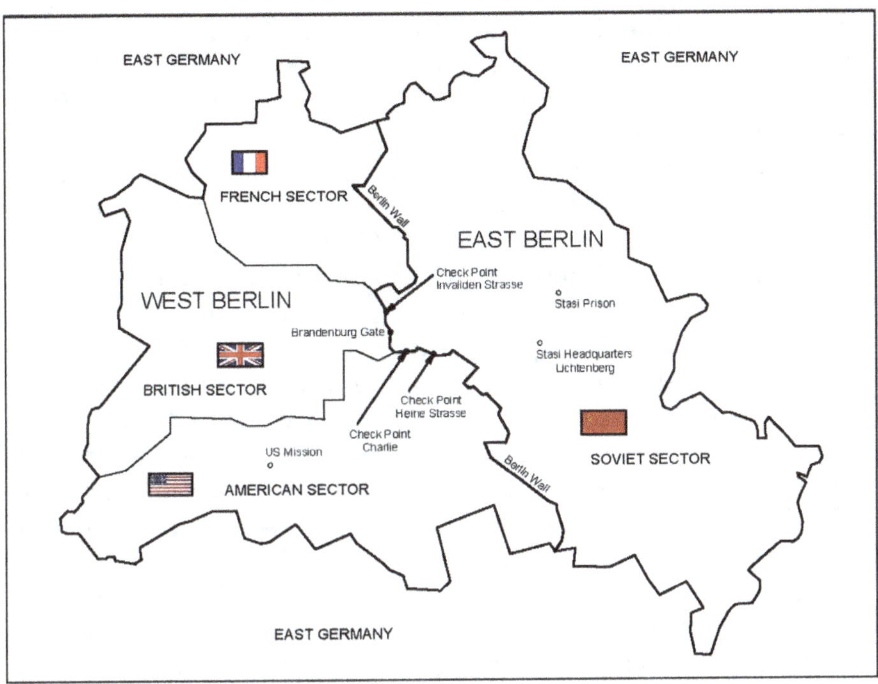

Berlin divided into three Allied sectors and the Soviet sector, all surrounded by the German Democratic Republic. The location of the US Mission, Stasi Headquarters, Hohenschönhausen prison and the border crossings from which the seven prisoners were released are depicted. Map drawing by Bernd Feuerherd.

concentrated efforts on stabilizing their occupied zones, the Soviets focused on reparations and dismantling the German industry to offset heavy wartime losses.[1]

In March 1948, in a tit-for-tat, the western Allies integrated their occupied zones without Soviet support. The Soviets retaliated by forming an East German state. Tensions escalated when a currency reform in the western zones, including West Berlin, introduced the Deutsche Mark against the will of the Soviet Union. The Soviets decided upon a blockade of West Berlin in June 1948.

The United States and Great Britain responded with a massive airlift, delivering supplies to the West Berlin population. These efforts generated overwhelming popular support. By the time the blockade was lifted in May 1949, the Soviets had suffered a major defeat and the Allies had formed the Federal Republic of Germany (FRG) or West Germany with its capital in Bonn. West Berlin, surrounded by the Soviet zone, retained its special status as a territory under Allied supervision.

Meanwhile in the Soviet German zone, the German People's Congress had drafted a constitution for a new East German state, modeled after the Soviet Union. The German Democratic Republic (GDR) was established on 7 October 1949, with East Berlin as its capital. The newly formed country instituted agrarian reforms by limiting land ownership and private trade and industry and focused on rebuilding its defunct heavy industry. High production quotas, meant to bolster the economy, however, had a crippling effect on the population and led to a mass exodus. Between 1949 and 1961, when the Wall was built, an estimated 3.5 million people fled to West Germany. Losing so many trained workers resulted in huge economic losses and severe manpower shortages in the GDR.[2]

Most refugees fled via West Berlin through its many crossing points; public transportation routes still connected both parts of the city. In fact, many East Berliners (*Grenzgänger*) worked in West Berlin and crossed the border daily, often deciding to move to the Western sector. The shrinking East Berlin labor force, higher work quotas and difficult living standards caused a disconnect between government officials and the public. Frustration led to strikes and demonstrations throughout East Germany in 1953.

The unrest began in East Berlin on 15 June 1953 when construction workers demanded an easing of new production quotas. They marched through the streets of the East German capital, attracting large crowds seeking political and social change. The GDR government was caught unprepared and ill-equipped. Moscow quickly took charge, ordering Soviet troops to restore order. The Soviets declared martial law on 17 June and closed the border one day later. While the uprising was quickly suppressed by the overwhelming Soviet military force, with many casualties and arrests, the consequences had lasting effects. Citizens were outraged that Soviet tanks had taken over German roads, and that the regime would defend its position so resolutely without offering meaningful reforms.

When the closed border led to food shortages, the United States started a 3-month food relief program, reaching 75 percent of the

East Berlin population.[3] This food program operated as a Cold War propaganda tool, since it was meant to destabilize East Germany and weaken the GDR regime.[4]

Additionally, citizen unrest resulted in the tightening of the East German Ministry for State Security, which transformed into one of the most coercive and effective security agencies in the Soviet bloc.[5] The connection between the GDR and the Soviet Union never wavered, even when Moscow granted sovereignty to the GDR in 1954. Moscow had military and economic interests to maintain, including the strategic placement of its advanced military position in the heart of Europe.

Two years after the 1953 uprising, in May 1955, West Germany joined NATO. During the same month, the Warsaw Pact, or Warsaw Treaty Organization, was founded as a political and military alliance between the Soviet Union and other Eastern European countries, including East Germany. The Warsaw Pact was meant to serve as a defensive alliance against the NATO. NATO and the Warsaw Pact in effect became counterweights to the spread of communism, forming a delineation between West and East.

Tensions between West- and East Berlin came to a head in 1958 when Soviet Premier Nikita Khrushchev delivered an ultimatum for the West to resolve the Berlin "problem" within six months. Khrushchev ordered the western Allies to withdraw from Berlin so that West Berlin could be turned into a "demilitarized free city."[6] Also, the Soviet Union and the East German regime wanted the Allies to deal with the GDR directly on all issues concerning the former Soviet zone.[7] Khrushchev's deadline passed without incident, but in June 1961, he reiterated his threat to sign a treaty with East Germany if the West did not come to an agreement concerning Berlin.

President John F. Kennedy responded on 25 July 1961, stating that the "western protecting powers have three essential interests in Berlin: 1. The right of the Allies to be in Berlin; 2. Their right of access to Berlin, and 3. The survival and right of self-determination of West Berlin."[8] Kennedy ordered a reinforced battle group from West Germany to move into West Berlin to show strength in force and clarify the American commitment to West Berlin.

East German workers reinforcing the Berlin Wall in October 1961 near the Brandenburg Gate, which divided the city starting August 13, 1961. United States Information Service, Department of State, https://research. archives.gov/description/6003284.

Barely one month later, the East Germans announced the closing of most border-crossings between East and West Berlin, leaving the Friedrichstrasse crossing in the American sector as the only Allied entry point into East Berlin.[9] No one foresaw what happened next. On 13 August, construction of what became the Berlin Wall began to keep East Germans from crossing to the West. Citizens were outraged, but the American response was guarded. The US was relieved that the Soviets had not signed a treaty with East Germany and that a direct confrontation with the Soviets had been averted. American officials considered the wall a "satisfactory stalemate: the Soviets did not challenge the legality of Allied rights, and the Allies did not challenge the reality of Soviet power."[10] Thereby the wall became a visual representation of the division of Europe, delineating the differences between communism and democracy.

As a precautionary measure, a permanent US military police detachment was stationed near the Friedrichstrasse crossing point in September 1961, called Checkpoint Charlie. After several notable stand-offs involving American and Soviet tanks, Checkpoint Charlie became an international symbol of opposition to the communist forces and the division of Berlin. US forces meanwhile patrolled the city's border to provide visible evidence of US military support for the West Berlin police.[11]

The allied occupied forces left their mark on West Berlin, not only in their military presence, but also in the landscape and culture. Shops and cinemas were built for the Allied forces, American and French cultural festivals were organized, and several prominent streets were renamed to honor allied generals. Growing prosperity led to a flourishing, artistic community and a thriving nightlife that benefited from a lack of curfew or mandatory closing times. Berlin became a magnet for the young and idealistic, seeking adventure. In many ways, the seven Americans, whose tales are depicted in this book, fit that niveau; they were young and idealistic, wanting to enjoy what Berlin had to offer, underestimating the dangers that awaited them when crossing into East Berlin.

Part One
Prisoner Stories

1

Photography with Consequences

"Would you please accompany me to headquarters to answer a few questions?" Such a simple question, from someone who looked like a "Sunday school teacher", changed Ronald Wiedenhoeft and our family's lives forever.[12]

Wiedenhoeft, an art and architectural history doctoral student and preceptor at Columbia University's Art History and Archaeology Department in New York City, had been photographing buildings in East Berlin for his dissertation, when he was approached by a man dressed in civilian clothes. Wiedenhoeft was studying housing projects designed by Bruno Taut, built in Berlin during the 1920s. Taut was a renowned German architect and urban planner, who became known for his theoretical works and his residential developments, many of which are now recognized as UNESCO World Heritage Sites. While it had been easy for Wiedenhoeft to access Taut's work in West Berlin, he was still missing vital information of Taut's housing developments in East Berlin.

Tuesday, 5 September 1967, was meant to be one of his final days in Berlin before returning to New York City for his fall semester studies. Wiedenhoeft had spent the last three months in Europe with his German-born wife, Renate, and their two young daughters, six-year-old Sonja, and one-year old Sabina. Our family lived with relatives in West Berlin and traveled throughout Europe. One year earlier, in 1966, my parents had started a business selling slides of art and architecture for teaching purposes to universities and museums. They had spent the summer months in Europe producing slides for the business, the sale of which would offset their travel expenses and provide income to their growing family. My father estimated that he had produced approximately three- or four thousand slides during the summer of 1967.[13] These photographs, produced between June and September 1967, were taken in Germany, Holland, Belgium, France, Switzerland, and Austria. After such a productive summer, my father now wanted to use his last remaining days in Berlin to focus on his doctoral studies.

Ronald Wiedenhoeft with his photography equipment in front of the Louvre Museum in Paris, August 1967. Curtesy Saskia Ltd.

Wiedenhoeft had enrolled at Columbia University two years earlier. Before the summer of 1967, he had completed all his course requirements and had passed his oral examinations, necessary for his doctor-of-philosophy degree, but he needed to complete his written dissertation. Professor Edgar Kaufmann of the History of Art and Architecture Department at Columbia University had suggested the topic of his study the previous year.[14]

Wiedenhoeft had excellent libraries with relevant material at his disposal. The Avery Library at Columbia University held the largest architecture resource collection in the US at the time, and the New York City Public Library as well as the Metropolitan Museum of Art provided invaluable resources for his studies. Additionally, Harvard University offered a wonderful collection of documents and media print by German architects. Nothing, however, replaced the value of seeing buildings in-situ. My father needed to visit and photograph as many of Bruno Taut's residential developments as possible.

Since there was no published material at the time which listed the locations of all Taut's projects and several street names had changed since the war years, he had to piece together the locations on his own. In West Berlin, he consulted the city planning office and the city library. Finding locations in East Berlin, however, was more elusive, since East and West Berlin did not share geographic information with each other. It wasn't even possible to purchase a current East Berlin map in West Berlin at the time.

My father had befriended a West Berlin architect by the name of Günter Meier, a proponent of modern architecture who owned a large collection of architectural magazines from the 1920s. In June 1967, he visited Meier to discuss his research, and the two men collaborated on hand-marking an older city map that included portions of East Berlin, which were included on a West Berlin map.[15] This map consisted of a series of localized map sections, each marked with a 4-digit number, for the user to piece together different sections of the Berlin metropolitan area.

Wiedenhoeft made notes of probable locations of the 14 sites he wanted to visit, and following the grid system of the maps, he made some additional notes concerning other map sections, which he wanted to consult later. "Before going over I'd worked up a list of developments I wanted to photograph. I had not actually visited them until that day. Since the city planning aspects of the developments were very important, I had to walk through them and get the feel of them; not just look at pictures. I didn't have their exact locations either. I did have a map cross hatched in the areas where the apartments were supposed to be and an architectural guide to the city written in 1931."[16] Wiedenhoeft's personal notes, including a reference to four additional map sections, were later confiscated by the Stasi. The Stasi initially claimed that the 4-digit map numbers corresponded to West Berlin phone numbers of known CIA and Allied military personnel[17].

During the morning hours of 5 September, my father left our family's Barstrasse apartment in West Berlin, made a few stops in West Berlin, then traveled by subway to East Berlin. He was the only passenger on the crowded subway to exit at Friedrichstrasse, near Checkpoint Charlie, around noon, giving him a somewhat ominous feeling right from the start. Emerging from the tunnel, he showed his American passport to a guard, filled out paperwork and made the mandatory five-mark currency exchange. He said: "I looked like the typical tourist with two camera bags and a tripod, even with luggage tags [from the airline] still attached".[18]

His aim was to photograph as many of the Bruno Taut housing developments in the most efficient manner. Initially, Wiedenhoeft headed to the northeastern part of East Berlin, to the Carl-Legien neighborhood and Buschallee, traveling by tram (S-Bahn) between areas. By mid-afternoon, he headed back south, towards the Lichtenberg area. He was eager to reach a large apartment development called Onnenhof by the German architect, Irwin Gautkind, which included a kindergarten in a park-like setting. On the way was a lesser-known Bruno Taut "rather cubistic, rectangular flat-roofed"[19] housing complex located along Normannenstrasse.

> I was interested because of these apartment developments of the 1920s represented a great change in the traditional way of housing in Berlin. I photographed them diagonally as I approached and again as I got a little closer. I had photographed these from the north side of Normannenstrasse and then I wanted to go around the buildings to

the south to get it from the back and I went into the side street which led south from Normannenstrasse and as I went on this street, there came what should have, I suppose, been a revelation to me. It should have told me to get the hell out of there because I saw a wall running down the street from right behind the houses going straight down south — a stucco stone wall, I guess — as I recall, it was just a plain white surface maybe 14 feet high or something like this. I just sort of felt well you know you're not going to take any pictures from this side. It looked like some sort of official complex or something and the only thing I thought was you're certainly not going to take any pictures around something like that.[20] [see map of area].

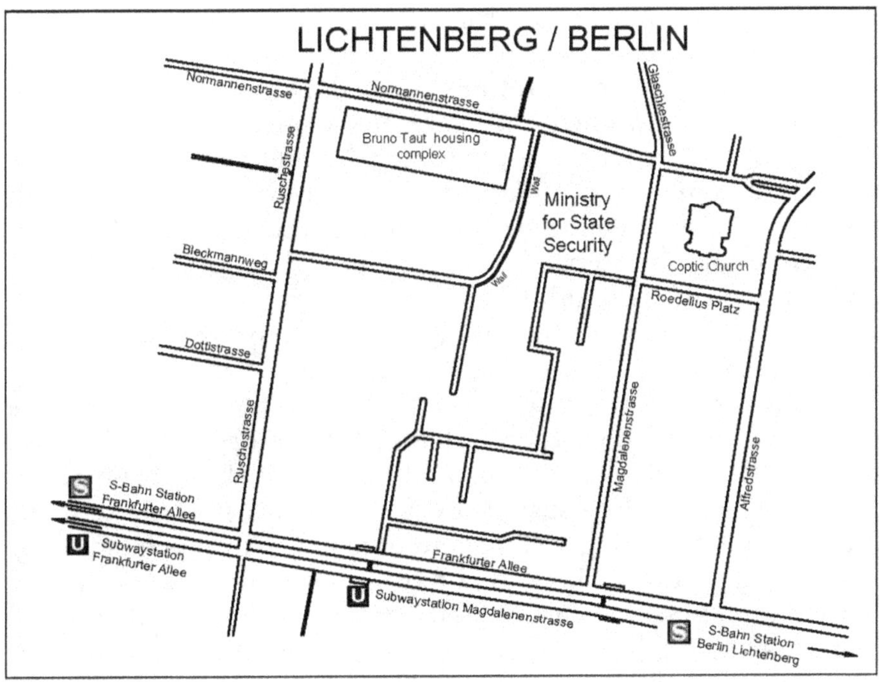

Map showing the route Wiedenhoeft took from the train station to the housing complex and its proximity to the Stasi headquarters. Map drawing by Bernd Feuerherd.

Unbeknown to Wiedenhoeft, behind that stucco wall was the Ministry for State Security. While there was a sign posted by the main entrance, there were no other obvious signs that the Ministry was housed there. Maps of East Berlin showed only a blank spot for the area and the building itself was not imposing and gave no indication of its significance.

While my father was busy photographing nearby, a Stasi informant by the name of GI "Kuba" was watching and reported him. GI "Kuba" was told to follow Wiedenhoeft, while two other agents, "Gen. Wählte" and "Gen. Großer", trailed behind, joining in the pursuit. They followed him as he walked towards Magdalenenstrasse, taking pictures of a historic church on Roedeliusplatz, before proceeding past the subway station Lichtenberg/ exit Frankfurter Allee to the S-Bahn train station Frankfurter Allee/Siegfriedstrasse. At that point, GI "Kuba" approached Wiedenhoeft, showed him his Stasi identification card, and asked Wiedenhoeft to accompany him for questioning.[21]

At first my father wasn't too worried, since he knew none of his photographs were of military installations or government buildings. He thought a few questions would clarify the matter. GI "Kuba" took him to a Trabant car, which was waiting for them around the corner with a driver. "He took me back to a building adjacent to the one I'd been photographing. I hadn't noticed it but on the façade of the building was a sign saying *Ministerium für Staatssicherheit* (Ministry for State Security). On most maps, including mine, the building was listed as a finance office."[22]

Inside, Wiedenhoeft was asked in a "very correct objective sort of way" what he had been doing, "I hadn't panicked because I knew I hadn't done anything, and I knew all about these apartments. They could be suspicious, but I could demonstrate that I knew what I was doing and that ought to have satisfied them. They kept saying just think how important this building is. I said 'Yes, but I haven't photographed it.' They took my films and developed them that night."[23] After several hours of questioning that went nowhere, my father was transferred again by Trabant car to the Hohenschönhausen prison where he was to spend the next nine months. Although interrogators questioned him until four the next morning before he was assigned to a cell, my father "still figured it would take time to check everything out, but in a day or so I'd be let out."

He was interrogated almost non-stop for the next two days. On the afternoon of the second day, he was called before a judge in the same building and had the order for his arrest read to him. He was charged with "having delivered information to imperialist secret services, with helping organizations who have smuggled people, and with customs and currency violations." In disbelief, Wiedenhoeft asked to have the charges repeated, "because it seemed so incredible. And then I just sort of laughed, and I said, 'What?! You mean murder isn't among the charges?'"[24]

Before he left the courtroom my father asked if he had the right to see a lawyer or the right not to answer questions. The judge answered no to both queries, adding "You're under a moral obligation to answer all questions." Under East German law, prisoners were not allowed legal counsel until their case was placed before the court. "You are not told of your few legal rights until it is too late."[25]

"They had never mentioned espionage before this. Never while I was there did they confront me with anything but the order for my arrest. They showed me the film they had developed the first night. Their building wasn't there. After that they sort of dropped the business of the photos."[26] "This is what really disturbed me, that they could have that attitude of just doing anything they damn pleased with me, taking my time, my freedom, just for the sake of writing down facts of my life."[27] And yet, recounting and writing down every detailed fact of Wiedenhoeft's life became his new daily prison routine.

Meanwhile, back in West Berlin, his wife (my mother) Renate was frantically trying to find her husband. When he did not return that first night, she and her sister-in-law, Emmy, came to East Berlin from her parents' home in West Berlin to look for him. Emmy had a Luxembourg passport, which allowed them entry into East Berlin, since West Berliners were not allowed to enter on their own. They filed a missing person report. The police checked the hospitals. Three days later, on 8 September 1967, my mother was brought to the East Berlin Prosecutor, General Joseph Streit, – the man who presumably had already signed the order for her husband's arrest – and he blandly denied knowing anything about it.[28]

Nor was there any official notice given concerning my father's disappearance. East German officials did not inform the American authorities. "We are quite concerned over this, as one would normally expect official notification in such a case," a spokesman said. "We view this detention as a blatant disregard of an individual… We shall continue to exert every effort we can to secure the release of Mr. Wiedenhoeft."[29] Normally, American officials would contact the Soviet Embassy in East Germany for information on missing US citizens, but those inquiries often remained unanswered.[30] A month later, the East German government finally released a statement regarding Wiedenhoeft's imprisonment. Robert J. McCloskey, the US State Department spokesman, made the following announcement. "The State Department has learned now that he [Wiedenhoeft] had been arrested in East Berlin on undetermined charges."[31]

2

Stasi Interrogation Tactics

Prisoners in East Germany were held under the jurisdiction of the Ministry for State Security (MfS), commonly known as the Stasi. The Stasi saw itself as the "sword and shield of the party", a slogan that reveals the unusual and omnipotent nature of the ministry. There is no mention of the people, the state, or the constitution in the slogan. According to their criminal code, the Ministry for State Security was an official investigative agency responsible for political cases, intelligence, and security concerns. That meant that in East Germany, the Socialist Unity Party (SED) and the MfS officiated over most political and security-related issues, thereby relegating the judiciary to an executor institution.[32] Official separation of powers did not exist; the East German regime considered law and justice the tools for building a communist society. The Stasi could therefore operate, to a certain extent, in a legal vacuum.[33]

Most Stasi employees were members of the SED party and saw themselves as the backbone of the communist state. Recruits were usually young men with a markedly low level of education. "Indoctrinated in political training schools, they absorbed the requisite ideas and mentally equipped themselves with the tools they needed for a lifelong orientation."[34] They became privileged members of an organization that held carte blanche with its monopoly on the secrecy of information, its suspension of human rights, and lack of oversight by courts and parliament. They operated without barriers in accessing private data which could be used for any purpose.[35] Stasi employees were rewarded for their loyalty with special privileges and higher salaries. They were also given the formal status of professional soldiers with a corresponding military rank.[36]

Party Secretary Erich Honecker congratulating Erich Mielke on the 30th anniversary of the Ministry for State Security, 8 February 1980. Bundesarchiv, Y 10-0097-91/ CC-BY-SA 3.0.

During the 1960s, the Stasi's leader was Colonel General Erich Mielke, who maintained this position until the collapse of East Germany in 1989. Mielke had a close affiliation with the SED party and yet made sure the party did not meddle in the Stasi's operative work.[37] He worked closely with party leaders and held regular private meetings with Walter Ulbricht (Party Secretary of the SED and Chairman of the GDR's State Council) and later Erich Honecker, Ulbricht's successor in 1971. Important political and operative matters were discussed during these meetings, but notes were never taken. "He [Mielke] continually pushed to have the ministry enlarged, to expand its areas of responsibility, to perfect its system of surveillance and to pursue psychological terror and persecution. He was also responsible for giving credence to the myth of the Stasi's omnipotence and omniscience."[38] Mielke's name became synonymous with the feared Stasi.

As early as 1961, the SED party issued a report criticizing the Stasi's methods and the extent of their power. However, the party offered no concrete reform plans and Mielke chose to ignore the criticism. The report cited the following complaints: "Arrests were made without judicial arrest warrants, house searches were conducted without orders from the public prosecutor and, as a result of its methods of appointment and informal relations, the public prosecutor was too closely involved with the MfS."[39] These unorthodox methodologies became standard practice and were maintained until the collapse of the regime. "The perception that surveillance and repression were omnipresent, the frightening immensity of the intelligence apparatus, the large number of prominent victims, and the deceptiveness of many of the Stasi measures"[40] came to define the East German security service.

The Stasi maintained the principle of double files with the official file containing legal material pertaining to the criminal proceedings, while a second, investigative file contained internal correspondences, operational documents and investigative reports that would shed light on the case. MfS regulations expressly denied the public prosecutor access to the investigative file, even though the prosecutor oversaw the complete investigative proceedings and the files contained significant information pertaining to the case. Also, prisoners generally were not allowed to see their legal counsel until after the MfS investigative proceedings had been concluded, making it essentially impossible to prepare an effective defense.[41] Stasi officials made sure they had complete power over the outcome of judicial proceedings concerning prisoners.

The Stasi's modus operandi was also known for its thoroughness in prisoner investigations. This level of detail started the moment a new prisoner arrived at a detention center. Uniformed guards photographed, finger- and palm-printed the prisoners, recorded any unique physical conditions, they weighed and measured the individual and confiscated their personal belongings after conducting an obligatory bodily search. A criminal file was then started on the prisoner with a prisoner identification number, even though they had not formally been charged yet.[42]

Street view of Hohenschönhausen Prison from Genslerstraße, 2018.
Author photo.

Foreign prisoners, such as Ron Wiedenhoeft, were mostly held
at Hohenschönhausen prison, located in a residential area near the
center of East Berlin. The existence of this prison was unknown
even to nearby residents. "Every street that leads in or out of the
area around it was blocked off by a boom gate and a sentry. Hohenschönhausen was a prison for political prisoners — it was the
innermost security installation in a secured area within a walled-off
country; it was another blank on the map.[43] Prisoners were not informed of their location. They were meant to feel helplessly subjected to the mercy of the almighty authority and completely cut-off
from the outside world.

The day after his arrest, Wiedenhoeft was put in pre-trial deten-
tion for suspected espionage charges. Berlin District Court Judge
Völlger signed the decree.[44] Lieutenant Günter Krenkel and Major
Wolfgang Plötner were assigned to be his interrogators.[45] After four

days of review, with no conclusive evidence, the initial interrogation was suspended.

All film material from my father's camera, including negatives, was confiscated and developed to determine whether any government buildings or military installations had been photographed. None were found. When he was arrested, Wiedenhoeft was carrying the following items: a 35mm camera, a tripod, several camera lenses, two camera bags with accessories, numerous film roles, a catalog of buildings in West- and East-Berlin (listing architects and construction dates), a city map with shaded, highlighted areas, a handwritten notebook, his American passport, his international student ID card, as well as other [non specified] papers. Officials determined that his passport was an unaltered, original document, and that listed names or addresses did not correspond to any known Stasi records. Further investigations by Soviet organizations also came back negative.

Interrogations concerning my father's identity also found nothing out of the ordinary. His teaching position at Columbia University and his dissertation topic, as well as his previous studies, were all confirmed. They determined that he had traveled 25 times from West Berlin into East Berlin in the past three years and in 1965 had spent several days visiting a family friend in Dresden, before continuing to Prague, Czechoslovakia.

Two items raised the interrogators' suspicion. One was Wiedenhoeft's notebook, containing notes pertaining to his photographs — the location, views, angles, shutter speed, exposure times. Even though his photographs matched his notes, GDR investigators were looking for hidden messages within the text. They also looked closely at Wiedenhoeft's city map. Some of the shaded areas, which my father had marked as locations for housing developments, were close to USSR military installations.

Reviewing all this material within only two days — this report was issued on 7 September 1967 — shows how vast the Stasi network was and how efficiently they worked, even without technological advances. The concluding report states that there was no reason to suspect that Wiedenhoeft had conducted any espionage activity or indeed violated any East German law. It recommended retaining all film material and personal notebook, releasing

Hallway with prison cells at Hohenschönhausen Prison in East Berlin, 2018. Author photo.

Wiedenhoeft from prison, and issuing a press release with the goal of "improved state sovereignty" for the GDR, thereby avoiding any possible smear campaign by Wiedenhoeft.[46]

If these recommendations had been followed, many hardships would have been avoided. Erich Mielke, the Stasi Minister, however, was not satisfied with some of the conclusions and wanted investigations to continue.[47] My father therefore was forced to settle into a prison routine, having no idea when or even if he would be released.

Hohenschönhausen prison consists of a U-shaped, three-story building, built by prisoners between 1959-61. Over 100 prison cells, housing one to four prisoners each, were in the north and east wings of the building, while 120 interrogation rooms were in the south wing. Prison cells were equipped with a wooden bed frame with mattress and blanket, a table and stool (both secured to the floor), a washbasin and a toilet. The walls were a two-toned brown and yellow and the floor a smooth, red, cement-like surface.

Wiedenhoeft was held in cell 165, from September 1967 until 19 January 1968. He shared this cell for eight weeks with an East German chemical engineer named Siegfried, who had tried to escape to the West. They got on very well and enjoyed discussing science, literature, music, and art. After Siegfried was moved to a different prison on 3 November, my father spent two weeks alone before Horst joined him in the cell on 19 November. Horst was an East German geodetic engineer who had supplied information to the CIA on business trips to West Germany.[48]

Prison cells had a double row of glass-blocks as a window, which allowed light and air to penetrate the cell. Wooden cell doors were steel-clad with a central flap for food delivery as well as a peephole for guards to watch the inmates round-the-clock. Usually, prisoners were given a prison uniform to wear, but my father was allowed to wear his own white shirt and trousers instead.

Bed linens were changed once a month, showers could be taken every Wednesday and three changes of water were provided each day to the cell. Wiedenhoeft's meals were surprisingly varied and plentiful. They were served on cafeteria-style trays with plates and silverware. This was another indication of my father's special treatment, since most prisoners had their meals served in plastic bowls without forks and knives.

Each morning, prisoners were allowed 30 minutes of fresh air and exercise in rectangular pens topped with barbed wire. Traveling between cell, outdoor pen or interrogation room was a highly controlled process. "As we entered the cell corridor, a guard turned on a switch that lit up big red stop lights on all sides and corners. I learned later that no one was let out of a cell until the lights were turned off. There would be no chance meetings of prisoners along the numerous corridors in this building. The floor of the corridor was covered with a plush red carpet, dulling the sound of footsteps. Along both walls at shoulder height hung tiny double alarm wires."[49]

My father was charged with "having delivered information to imperialist secret services, with helping organizations who have smuggled people, and with customs and currency violations." However, when the initial investigations failed to uncover proof of these accusations, the Stasi formulated a procedural plan to substantiate their claims. They developed an "assessment of the process" in which reference was made to other cases involving Americans charged with espionage. Similarities to other cases were cited and recommendations were made to follow similar procedural methodologies with Wiedenhoeft. Their goal was to prove that my father "had been a secret intelligence agent for many years; that his cover in East Germany had been carefully planned; his employment as an art historian was a cover and served as a structure for his espionage activities; his mission was carefully planned in connection with the secret service; that he took part in smuggling activity; that he served as liaison officer for smugglers; that he helped plan smuggling activity; and that he transported objects illegally on his entries into the GDR."[50]

Investigators started with a character analysis of Wiedenhoeft. They determined that he had "a balanced, calm personality with a particularly strong emotional life... He represents the image of an apolitical scientist with a pacifist worldview." They took into consideration that as an American, his "life principles" would be different from theirs, and took note of how his family background, career choices and lifestyle had shaped who he was. More importantly, since Wiedenhoeft had categorically denied all allegations, the Stasi determined that it was paramount to conduct all interrogations as factually as possible, avoid direct accusations and take careful notes for later cross-examinations. All political discussions, such as the Vietnam war or race problems, were to be avoided. They even stipulated guidelines always to follow precision and order, "since the accused attaches great importance to cleanliness."

Since a confession by my father was deemed unlikely, they were determined to "break the physical and psychological resistance of [the accused], as this is the only way to achieve results." They wanted to make Wiedenhoeft mull over their questions, while the interrogator showed no compassion, understanding or offered any commentary.

The character analysis extended to a factual assessment of childhood events, contacts, and upbringing. The Stasi wanted to know every mundane detail: why he had chosen certain subjects in school and university, which lectures he attended at the university level, list all his contacts ranging from personal friendships, family members, colleagues, and professionals. They even questioned my father on why he received two Fulbright scholarships to study in Germany and whether the CIA could have granted him this special privilege. Financial circumstances were analyzed in detail as were possible political influences in his daily life.

Of special interest was any connection to East German citizens, particularly employees of the Bode Museum in East Berlin, where Wiedenhoeft had photographed on numerous occasions. Was Wiedenhoeft posing as an art historian to photograph East German military installations for the CIA? The fact that my father had brought 3-4 books, chocolate, and coffee to employees at the Bode Museum as thank you gifts served as proof that he had violated customs and foreign exchange laws.

Wiedenhoeft was interrogated in a room equipped with a desk and chair for the interrogator, along with a phone and typewriter. A filing cabinet and another cabinet containing hidden listening devices filled the room. He sat on a stool in the corner, rather than across from the interrogator at the desk. That space was reserved for signing documents or for special privileges, such as receiving a cup of coffee. Surprisingly, my father was often asked if he would like to have coffee and cake during his interrogation sessions. Even more surprising, his wishes were usually granted.

At first, he was told the investigation would take three months (the usual length for interrogations in East Germany), then six months, and finally a year. The flexible provisions of the East German criminal code allowed the Stasi to criminalize almost any behavior and gave investigators the power to decide how prisoners were treated. "The interrogator had the power to decide on disciplinary measures, tougher sentencing, provisions of medical care, providing reading and writing material, and granting exercise privileges or allowing visitors.[51]"

"It was a topsy-turvy world," Wiedenhoeft said. "The more you would explain, the more they thought you were covering something up."[52] Five days a week, he was questioned from 8 am until 5 pm, with a lunch break. He was interrogated by Lieutenant Krenkel regarding personal matters, such as family background and people he knew in Berlin and East and West Germany. He was also required to retrace, step-by-step, all his 25 previous visits to

East Berlin as well as his visits to Dresden and Prague during the summer of 1965. Detailed, daily notes were taken, which my father had to later review and sign.

The lieutenant was very pedantic in recording all conversations. As my father later recalled: "This was sort of a frustrating thing, you know, to think that they could take something and make a big deal out of nothing... This is what really disturbed me, that they could have that attitude of just doing anything they damn pleased with me, taking my time, my freedom, just for the sake of writing down facts of my life."[53] Of course, this was part of their interrogation plan; piecing together a character analysis, looking for inconsistencies and hoping to trip the prisoner when they would later return to cross-examine the same material. Would Wiedenhoeft answer the questions similarly? He was not allowed to have any writing material in his cell, to avoid summarizing his thoughts at the end of each day.

Meanwhile, my father was also wondering if he should really answer all these seemingly irrelevant questions. After all, why should he tell them about things that had no connection to the accusations?

Also, his Western mentality was making him second guess the right approach. "I mean it is the most basic reasoning to think that anything you say might be held against you." Then again, if he refused to answer questions, would it raise more suspicion by not cooperating? Also, he couldn't help feeling annoyed by the amount of time these questions were taking. Knowing that his conscience was clear, and he was powerless, he decided to cooperate fully with the hope they would soon realize their mistake. Of course, this reasoning was what the Stasi interrogators had counted on. "This set-up achieved strong, mental stress which often led to wanting to communicate with the interrogator and promoted the wish to cooperate and testify. This was linked with the entire repertoire of sophisticated interrogation techniques: alternate between showing great sympathy, followed by pressure tactics and threats."[54]

Some of the questions focused on art history knowledge. Wiedenhoeft was given an art history book with illustrations of paintings, which he was asked to critique. The interrogator also tested his general art history knowledge. During one such session, the lieutenant tried to rile my father by making fun of Francisco Goya's painting "The Third of May 1808", in which Goya commemorated the Spanish resistance to Napoleon's armies in the Peninsular War. The exasperated lieutenant called it a ridiculous painting and stammered: "You weird and pathetic art historian, you..."

What Wiedenhoeft didn't realize was that by being an art historian — and an academic — he made himself look guilty. In one report, his reviewing officer drew comparisons to a CIA agent who had received instructions from an American professor at an international scientific conference held in East Berlin[55]. There were other well-known cases of spies who were art historians. Anthony Blunt, the Cambridge University art historian turned spy, had made international headlines in 1964, after being offered immunity from prosecution for confessing to being a Soviet spy. By strange coincidence, Blunt had befriended the German art historian Rudolf Wittkower, who later emigrated to the United States and became the chairman of the Art History and Archaeology Department at Columbia University — the very same department where my father was a preceptor.[56]

Wittkower had even written a letter of support for my father, in October 1967. In the letter, he confirmed that Wiedenhoeft was "a devoted scholar and his pursuits were, and are, solely concerned with academic matters."[57] Additionally, Professors Collins and Kaufman, Wiedenhoeft's major advisors at Columbia University, had stated their willingness to testify in a trial on his behalf, while Grayson Kirk, the President of Columbia University, wrote a letter addressed to Walter Ulbricht (the SED Party Secretary and Chairman of the GDR's State Council), asking him to exert his influence to see that justice was done.

Another unknowingly incriminating aspect of my father's detention was his calm, collected demeanor and sharp memory, befitting a trained spy. He never lost his calm, resorted to yelling or refused to cooperate. He tried to reason with his interrogators, asking how they could imprison someone without any proof. They replied that he was being held for questioning, not imprisoned, even though that argument seemed arbitrary. When Wiedenhoeft objected to the subject matter of their questions, he was simply met with blank stares. They also considered his friendship with two American military intelligence officers (whom he had befriended in high school) as proof of his intelligence connections.

Later, during his interrogation sessions with the major, the term "cultural espionage" was used to describe what Wiedenhoeft had done. As my father understood it, that term referred to someone obtaining societal information, observing the attitude of people and how society functions to report those observations to Western information agencies. "Things that we would consider intellectual curiosity", as my father later pointed out with frustration.

By the end of November 1967, the investigation entered a new phase. Major Plötner took the place of Lieutenant Krenkel. "He did nothing except every day, five days a week, he kept talking to me and telling me I ought to confess, that they knew everything." The major tried to entrap him with questions that couldn't be answered properly, such as "who do you know that wanted to leave the German Democratic Republic?" The aim was to break Wiedenhoeft; to make him feel like he had failed to answer the questions properly, thereby indicating his disinclination to cooperate. "He kept saying: We never make any mistakes. We never have yet. We've never arrested anybody who was not guilty."

And yet, my father was surprised by the politeness of most Stasi officers. Basic wishes were usually granted and the major even rose to greet Wiedenhoeft each time he entered the interrogation room, shaking hands at the beginning of each session, offering coffee and cake around 10 am. Since the major didn't take any notes and spent most of his time just listening to my father answer questions while smoking cigarette after cigarette, Wiedenhoeft started smoking just to have something to do.

"They treated me in a rather civilized, almost friendly manner, in this early stage, getting this handshake business every day, asking whether I would like coffee and cake." With cooler temperatures in the fall and my father still wearing his summer clothes, which were getting rather worn, he asked for a sweater. Instead, he received a new, navy sweat suit, white dress shirt and pants. "I seemed to be getting special treatment, in that I didn't have to wear this striped prison pajama as a shirt or as underwear." When asked, prison guards also washed and returned Wiedenhoeft's own clothes to him in the cell.

Prisoners could borrow books from a library on a weekly basis. A guard came around with a list and would let prisoners select up to four books at a time. The list included German classic literature and even some American authors (translated into German), such as Erskine Caldwell and Mark Twain (both were favorites behind the Iron Curtain since they dealt with some of the worst aspects of American life). Wiedenhoeft and his cellmates made good use of this resource, but when they ran out of books to read, his wish to have his own architectural guidebook (which he had with him when he was arrested) was granted. Later he was also given an Italian-German dictionary, after expressing his wish to improve his Italian and French skills.

When my father complained to the major that it was hard to read by the dim light in their cell, arrangements were made to move the cellmates to a larger, brighter cell on 19 January 1968. Cell 133 was a spacious room with three beds, located in the north wing, near the guard barracks. It had a wooden table on which previous occupants had scratched a chessboard pattern. Since my father and his cellmate Horst had collected apple and cherry seeds from snacks they received in their previous cell, they used those seeds to play chess and Chinese checkers to pass the time. Sometimes they could hear faint sounds from the television in the guard's barracks broadcasting the Winter Olympics or music from the radio.

Evenings, at nine pm, lights were turned off for the prisoners and the guards. My father could sometimes hear Mozart's lullaby "Sleep, my little Prince, Sleep" (*Schlafe, mein Prinzchen, Schlaf ein*) or the Italian Taps (*Il Silenzio*) being played over the P.A. system to lull the guards to sleep. Listening to the music in bed, while holding photographs of his wife and children, Wiedenhoeft felt like he was in the executive prison suite.

One of Wiedenhoeft's fervent wishes, however, was not granted. Since September, he had asked to write a letter to his wife, Renate. In November he was allowed to write a short letter of reassurance, but the letter was rejected by the state attorney on a technicality and never posted. My mother's weekly letters, family photographs and care packages, sent over the nine-month period, never reached him. Even an Easter greeting drawn by his six-year-old daughter, Sonja, was sent to be analyzed for possible hidden messages and never forwarded. Not until the end of April were correspondence privileges finally granted, one month before Wiedenhoeft's release.

In some ways, my father felt grateful for his daily interrogation sessions. It passed the time and gave him the feeling that he wasn't forgotten, and that progress could still be made. He was never asked to perform manual labor, even though that was considered a standard practice for prisoners in East Germany. The East German economy depended on this free labor, since there was a constant labor shortage and goods produced by prisoners were exported to the West for much needed hard currency.[58]

All information gathered wasn't just to solve a case of supposed espionage. The Stasi were interested in collecting information of all kinds. Wiedenhoeft was being used as an information supply about the West. Any little detail could be considered significant. He was basically asked to explain every single move that he had ever made. If my father claimed not to remember certain aspects, or not to be able to explain why he had done a certain thing, they never accepted that. "Their attitude is that everything you do has a reason, and if you think about it long enough and explain it, this will become obvious, you know, what your reason was, and that it was logical and rational." This was a new way of thinking for Wiedenhoeft and made for many frustrating discussions.

My father also discovered that the East Germans were very interested in people — the science of studying personalities. They were analyzing him, always probing deeper, wanting explanations for everything. "They kept talking in this seemingly rational, logical, reasonable method, as intelligent people, and always saying that, you know, that they have nothing to gain by holding anyone who hasn't done anything, and, you know, the fact of my being held there, at the same time, said just exactly the opposite — that they're irrational, they're illogical, they don't know what they're doing, and it was just so stupid."

Wiedenhoeft felt their methodology was not illogical. In fact it was quite reasonable, but they were basing their presumptions on what they wanted to believe rather than on facts and they were too focused on proving their superiority. "They constantly tried to break down your confidence in your own system and build up theirs as eminently reasonable and rational and kind, generous, not that they tried to convert me to Communism at all, but they were certainly always presenting themselves in a good light." Individual rights did not hold value in East Germany. "They play up the system for the good of mankind in the abstract form rather than in the individual."

No matter what my father told his interrogators, there was no convincing them of his innocence. In fact, they would ask: "Did anyone ever tell you that you had to prove your innocence?" And yet, the major liked to stress that it would be in Wiedenhoeft's best interest to confess and clear his mind. One German proverb he liked to use was: "A clear conscience is a soft pillow."[59]

Normally the weekends were quiet, with no interrogation sessions and prisoners remaining in their cells. In mid-January, however, my father was in for a surprise. On Saturday, 20 January, he was unexpectedly brought in from the exercise pen to a new corner office where he was met by an elderly gentleman dressed in Western clothes, "clearly some sort of high official". This official tried the fatherly approach to gain a confession for the sake of family responsibilities. He indicated that he had investigated Wiedenhoeft's case, told him he was guilty and should realize a confession was the only reasonable solution under the circumstances.

When my father replied that he had nothing to confess, the gentlemen raised his voice: "There is nothing questionable about this investigation. Everything stands firm and this has been a really clean piece of work. They have checked out everything, and it stands perfectly clear that you're guilty. I'm going to tell you that when your daughters (6 and 1 years old) are ready to get married you'll still be sitting here. We won't let you out of this house… Try to overcome your cowardice and make the big decision, you know; really show some courage."

Wiedenhoeft got the impression that they were hinting at making a deal with him. If only he would be more reasonable and offer to assist them in some fashion, perhaps with an assignment in the West, they could reach an agreement and he would be released. Hints were made, but no one asked him directly. They wanted to settle the matter as "intelligence officers" (*Berufskollegen*). They never referred to spying by name, only as "our profession". The CIA was also never mentioned by name, only as "our competition."

After the unexpected meeting with the official, interrogation sessions with the major continued. A few weeks later, in mid-February, my father was in for another surprise. One morning, three prison guards entered his cell, asked the men to stand against the wall and proceeded to make a thorough inspection of the cell. They tore everything apart and collected all personal belongings, including books, photographs, even the table with the checkerboard scratched on it. Wiedenhoeft and his cellmate were no longer allowed to sit or lie on their beds during the day, and their reading privileges were revoked. It felt like a hazing, "maybe putting you in your place by making you realize that you shouldn't have it too good and that there is a higher authority that can do whatever he wants."

This turn of events signaled the start of the third phase of interrogation for my father. He went from enjoying lots of amenities to having them all taken away. Even his daily interrogations stopped for a time, leaving him to sulk in his cell and exert maximum pressure by isolating him. When he was finally called back to the interrogation room, the major had changed his tune and was no longer willing to be friendly or accommodating. He asked: "Do you have something more to add?" When my father didn't offer anything new, he was returned to his cell to contemplate his situation. "I felt that some higher-up official must be putting pressure on him [the major] for not getting anything more positive out of me." The major got nervous and tense, losing his composure and getting nastier, accusing Wiedenhoeft of being one of the worst prisoners. After trying the softer approach without desired results, a harsher, nastier tone was taken.

In early March, a visit from the state attorney was announced. The state attorney said the evidence against Wiedenhoeft proved his guilt and that the investigation would be extended from six months to a year, until September 1968. After the state attorney left, the major started dictating all their conversations into a tape recorder, asking Wiedenhoeft detailed questions about Columbia University, students protesting the CIA recruiting tactics on campus, the race riots, and political leanings of professors. He asked about scholars in the West who had contracts in communist nations. "They seemed paranoid about East-West contact, especially professional contacts."

One line of questioning focused on the role of art in contemporary society. Could expressionism, an artistic style of art depicting subjective emotions and responses as opposed to reality, be useful in modern society? Communist societies tended to focus on art simply for the glorification and enlightenment of the working classes. Being asked to engage in such philosophical discussions frustrated my father since he didn't see the point of it. And yet, the major liked to point out that everything had a reason. If a person thinks about something long enough, the explanation for any action will become obvious in a rational manner. This argument was also used whenever Wiedenhoeft voiced frustration at having to remember too many mundane daily facts.

While not every conversation was recorded into the protocol, my father could not let down his guard, since any careless comment he made could and would be endlessly analyzed and discussed. The major kept repeating that they never made any mistakes – that when they arrested a person, he was always guilty and that if he ever went to trial, he would certainly be convicted."[60]

While my father was never tempted to make a false confession, the endless discussions were exhausting and disheartening. As he later recalled: "I did get depressed, of course. But I always had hope, and it was sort of intellectually stimulating to have this constant repartee, and I was always tempted to give them sort of sarcastic remarks or, you know, witty comments back."

Was it naive or idealistic to think nothing could happen if no crime had been committed? By early April, Wiedenhoeft started to think there might be an end in sight. There seemed to be nothing new to discuss and he was getting hopeful that he could be released by early summer, possibly even in time for my, his younger daughter, Sabina's, second birthday on 4 June. On 24 April, he was given permission to write to his wife, even though he hadn't pressed the matter for several months. His privileges of reading, sitting, and lying on bed were also reinstated after he asked for it.

Unbeknown to my father, Erich Mielke, head of the Stasi, personally signed his release form on 27 May. Around the same time, Major Platter casually asked Wiedenhoeft if he was getting enough fresh air and offered to take him on an outing over the Pentecostal holiday weekend (in early June). To prepare for this outing, he offered to have a whole new wardrobe fitted for Wiedenhoeft (from underwear, suit, shirt, tie, socks, even shoes). The major then announced that Wiedenhoeft should be ready to leave early Monday morning, 3 June. My father could tell that something had changed in the atmosphere.

Monday morning, he was given his new clothes to wear and brought to the major who was waiting for him with coffee and cake. The major asked if Wiedenhoeft had anything further to contribute to his story. When my father said he had nothing to offer, the major asked him for any special wishes. Wiedenhoeft replied he wanted to get back to his wife and family, simply to be free again. With a sly smile, the major responded: "Well, okay. Agreed." The major also told him he was lucky to be released, because he could have expected a 15-year sentence if he had been brought to trial.[61]

Before his release, Wiedenhoeft had to write a statement confirming he had been treated fairly. He also received his personal belongings, minus the confiscated items, thereby releasing the Stasi from any further demands. My father later mulled: "I certainly would have claims if they would compensate me for these nine months of unjust incarceration, but that didn't occur to me in that moment of excitement."

Wiedenhoeft and the major were driven in a prisoner transport van to the MfS headquarters before proceeding to meet his American lawyer. It was to be my father's first meeting with a lawyer. He never met Wolfgang Vogel, his East German lawyer. Wiedenhoeft was brought to the Unter den Linden Hotel where he was offered champagne and later met Maxwell Rabb, his American lawyer, with his son, Bruce. The elder Rabb had brought his son, a fellow lawyer, along in case anything went awry, and he could send his son to report back to the West. The Rabbs were in a hurry to get back to the West. After a short car ride, they were dropped off at Checkpoint Charlie and walked through the border crossing without having to show any papers.

Within a few minutes, they were met by an official from the US Mission in West Berlin, along with the head of the Public Security for the American sector of Berlin and a photographer from the *Stars and Stripes* publication, who took photos of Wiedenhoeft and the Rabbs at the Checkpoint. There was no debriefing at the Mission afterwards, only a request for a press conference for the next day to appease the international press. My father was told: "Now you're free, you're a completely free agent. Our job is done and we're happy that it's done, and we don't have anything more, any demands of you."

3

The Story of Five American Prisoners

In 1964, three years before Ron Wiedenhoeft's arrest, John van Altena, a twenty-year-old American student from Wisconsin, was apprehended at Checkpoint Charlie, trying to smuggle an East German mother and daughter across the border. On 8 October 1964 van Altena attempted to drive his American Ford across the border with the woman and child hidden in secret compartments.

Van Altena had been living in Hamburg since March 1964. He was planning on studying law at the Free University in Berlin starting in November of that year. Wanting to earn money in the meantime, his fluency in German, English and Spanish had landed him a job with Lufthansa Airlines at the Fuhlsbüttel Airport in Hamburg. There, he befriended Werner Kloss, who had a married cousin living in East Germany. This cousin, Jürgen Rabe, together with his wife Bärbel and their four-year-old daughter Sabrina, wanted to escape to West Germany. Moved by their story and wanting to help his friend, van Altena offered to help execute a plan to free the young family. They worked on an escape plan for two months. When their first idea of traveling through Hungary proved impossible, van Altena agreed to drive the concealed passengers across the Berlin border in an altered vehicle.

The idea was to use a large foreign car with custom plates, which were generally restricted to foreign tourists buying a car and having it shipped overseas. Since cars with custom plates were usually excluded from a detailed border inspection, the plan seemed safe.[62] Van Altena had chosen a 1959 American Ford for its extraordinarily large gas tank. The compartment was wide enough to hold the four-year-old after he rebuilt the trunk bottom.

For the adult passenger, John found a 14-inch partition between the trunk and the back seat. He cut out part of the hull over the differential from fender to fender and lowered it by four inches. He then created an additional three inches of width by shortening the coil springs in the back seat, creating just enough space for one person to fit in the space. Additionally, the fuel line was rerouted, and a rubber mat was added to cushion the tight compartment. Several concealed latches under the seat were used for loading and unloading the passengers.[63]

A tip-off, however, changed van Altena's careful plans. As he approached the border crossing, he noticed there were about twice as many guards as usual. After he was asked to step out of the car and his passport was taken, five guards started an unusually thorough and detailed search of the vehicle. Although the guards initially found nothing suspicious, van Altena was told to drive the car to a control house, where he was asked to stand against a wall with his hands up. While guards continued to tear the car apart, a body search of van Altena was conducted and a pistol, concealed under his jacket, was discovered. Although the woman and child in the car had not yet been found, van Altena was promptly arrested. Carrying a weapon in East Germany was illegal. "In East Germany, private gun ownership was outlawed."[64] Even privately-owned hunting rifles were locked up at hunting clubs, with access restricted to prearranged times. Schooling and licensing were required, and every bullet had to be accounted for — hit or miss.[65]

Later, when van Altena was questioned about his background and connections, he failed to mention his Peace Corps training, which he had completed during the summer of 1963, before attending the University of Wisconsin. The Peace Corps program had been created by President John F. Kennedy in 1961. The principles of nation building and promoting democracy abroad were counter to the communist mentality and therefore strongly opposed by the East German regime. "To the East Germans it is a subversive organization, infiltrated by the CIA, working under the mask of helping develop the so-called underdeveloped countries."[66] Any connection to the Peace Corps raised suspicion and anger from the MfS. When the investigation also uncovered a close family friend who had escaped Czechoslovakia in 1955, van Altena was placed in solitary confinement.[67]

For the next several months, van Altena was held in cell 45 at Hohenschönhausen prison. While treated politely by the guards, he was not granted special privileges, nor was he given any special meals. To exert psychological pressure, his nights were interrupted with lights turning on every ten minutes.[68] During the day, a major and a captain alternately asked van Altena to account for every month of his life since turning sixteen. Van Altena refused to cooperate, not wanting to endanger his friends, and fearing inconsistent stories with Bärbel Rabe, who was also incarcerated at Hohenschönhausen. Twelve days after van Altena's arrest Jürgen Rabe was arrested. Despite being told of his friend's arrest, van Altena still refused to cooperate with his interrogators. In early November, the two men were brought face to face. The tactic worked in part since Rabe made a full confession.

To build a defensive wall around himself, van Altena developed a pose of "a cocky, smug, sneering punk kid."[69] This mask helped him hide his fears and insecurities. In December 1964, the major questioned van Altena intensively on the Peace Corps. The major was interested in the type of training van Altena had received, especially his training in communism (or anticommunism as he pointed out), the effectiveness of the Corps' work as well as the newly developed West German Peace Corps. The major made it clear that van Altena's Peace Corps training would be used in his trial to prove that he had been trained in "subversive" thoughts on anticommunism.[70]

Around the same time, in mid-December, van Altena was suddenly told he would meet his East German lawyer, Friedrich Karl Kaul. He was brought to the Magdalenen Street prison for the meeting since no visitors were allowed to enter Hohenschönhausen prison. The lawyer was a short, heavy-set, balding man in his sixties. Kaul, a prominent government lawyer, was a staunch Communist. Much to van Altena's surprise, Kaul began to lecture him on foreigners having to respect the laws of the country they visit and recommended that he level with the Stasi.[71]

Shortly thereafter, van Altena was moved from Hohenschönhausen prison to Bautzen II prison in Saxony, near the Czech-Polish border. Bautzen was one of East Germany's prison towns, with three prisons. Bautzen II prison was the only East German prison under direct MfS control. It was "a really nasty, old place" with

Prison cell with bunkbeds at the Stasi owned prison Bautzen II, near the Czech-Polish border, 2015. Photo Fiver, der Hellseher.

primitive facitilites.[72] There, van Altena shared cell 13 with an East German named Gerhard. On 21 December, he was brought to the District Attorney who told him he was being charged with persuading GDR citizens to leave the country illegally and for carrying a firearm.[73] On 2 January 1965, van Altena was sentenced to "one year for illegal possession of weapons and seven and one-half years maximum security at hard labor for the smuggling of GDR citizens". This was later rounded off to eight years of hard labor.[74]

While van Altena did not actually perform any labor, he lost around 20 pounds from the tasteless, monotonous food he received. The lack of nutrients and proteins in his diet affected his health. While he tried to stay active by doing push-ups and knee-bends in his cell, by September 1965, his muscles had weakened to such an extent that he started to limp. When he later tore a tendon in his right foot, the poor medical treatment he received only made matters worse.

A break-through came five months later, in February 1966, when van Altena was finally able to meet his new East German lawyer, Wolfgang Vogel, who had taken on his case eleven months earlier. The van Altena family in Wisconsin had fired attorney Kaul, based on an assessment from the State Department that Kaul had failed to make significant progress. Van Altena was amazed by Vogel's appearance. "Vogel looked very young, almost like a student. He had on expensive, fashionable clothes, and wore his hair closely cropped. It was hard to believe this young man was a highly respected representative of the East German government trusted by both sides, but when he began to speak, I could tell he was experienced and self-assured."[75] Vogel made it clear that his case was very difficult; however, he had managed to arrange a joint meeting with Ricey J. New Jr., van Altena's American lawyer.

A prisoner meeting with his East and West lawyers was a novelty. Van Altena explained: "The GDR officials had permitted something in my case that had never been done before in a foreign case. If everything went as planned, I would be allowed a visit from New, my Washington lawyer. ... As an American lawyer, New had no authority, but the fact that he could visit me indicated a thaw in the case."[76] New, a governmental lawyer from Washington, DC had worked with the East-West team, Wolfang Vogel and Jürgen Stange, on several cases, including the much publicized 1962 case involving the exchange of Francis Gary Powers, the American U-2 pilot shot down by the Soviets, and the Soviet spy Rudolf Abel in 1962.

When New met van Altena on 4 February 1966, he brought a *New York Tribune* article to show van Altena that New and Vogel had worked on previous cases together. The article contained a list of all Americans currently imprisoned in East Germany. New asked if van Altena knew any of them, thereby hinting they were working to free all of them. "Most of the conversation was in German between Vogel and me. ... He (Vogel) spoke very little English and New spoke no German."[77] Vogel mentioned a possible April release date for van Altena.

After this hopeful meeting, van Altena was unaware of further negotiations on his behalf, until his sudden release on 16 March 1966. One day his East German major slyly asked, "John, how would you like to have a beer in West Berlin tonight?" The Major explained that Walter Ulbricht (the Socialist Unity Party Secretary and Chairman of the GDR's State Council) had pardoned van Altena for good behavior and had placed him on parole.[78] Later, van Altena learned: "By word of the First Party Secretary my sentence had been found too high and revised to two and one-half years, which made it possible for them to release me on good behavior after having served half of this new sentence, the minimum prescribed by East German law."[79]

The fact that the American lawyer, Maxwell Rabb, had worked on his behalf first became apparent once van Altena met Rabb in Vogel's office. "He [Vogel] introduced me to Maxwell Rabb, a distinguished man in a black wool suit. He was obviously an American and looked like an embassy official. Vogel immediately left us alone. You can't imagine how wonderful it is to see you, John, he [Rabb] whispered, closing my hands tightly. He simply said that he was the man who had been responsible for my release and that we had to get out of there quickly. He spoke no German and I found my English difficult to handle."[80]

Leaving the Eastern sector with Rabb and Vogel proved memorable. Van Altena and Rabb were transported by Vogel in his Mercedes through the Invaliden Street crossing, usually reserved for East German officials. Vogel joked: "I'll show you how to take money, anything, over the border. This is how you should smuggle people out. Watch closely." Even Rabb was in on the joke, saying: "Watch this, John. This will show you who Vogel really is." As they neared the high cement wall and barbed wire surrounding the checkpoint, heavily armed guards were standing at attention. Vogel did not slow down, as two guards saluted them, and they raced through the first barrier. With squealing tires, Vogel continued through the slalom course of heavy cement blocks until they passed through the West German border. "I looked at Vogel in amazement, then turned around and just smiled at Rabb. It had been a spectacular crossing. ... Rabb was suddenly full of questions. It was his first time on such a case. He wanted to know what my feelings were now that I was a free man."[81]

After this success, Rabb, as President of the United States Committee for Refugees, invited John van Altena to be the guest of honor at the Committee's annual dinner in Washington, DC, where Vice President Hubert H. Humphrey gave the keynote address.[82] There, van Altena heard about the intricate negotiations that had taken place on his behalf; how Rabb had — at his own initiative and expense — made four trips to East Germany to untangle the "snarls left by the earlier negotiations". "The manner in which my release was effected — without an exchange of prisoners or cash — was unprecedented."[83] Van Altena later wrote a book detailing his tribulations from his family home in Wisconsin before returning to West Germany to complete his law degree. He maintained a close affiliation with the FRG throughout his professional life. For many years, as a German teacher in Wisconsin, he eagerly led student trips to Berlin, enlightening a new generation to the Cold War tensions of the divided city.

After van Altena's release, the celebration for Maxwell Rabb was short-lived. He was soon approached by the State Department to lend his expertise in negotiating the release of four other Americans held in East German prisons: William Lovett, Frederick Matthews, Moses Herrin, and Mary Hellen Battle. All four were arrested during 1965.

Twenty-four-year-old William Lovett, from San Francisco, California, was apprehended on 8 May 1965, following a traffic accident in Leipzig with a school bus. "Mr. Lovett was reported to have caused the accident, in which several children sustained light injuries and an adult passenger was hurt severely."[84] Lovett had travelled by car from West Germany to Leipzig, in East Germany, accompanied by Jasminca Tkalac, from Yugoslavia, at the time of the accident. Just like John van Altena, Lovett had carried a concealed weapon.

Lovett's two offenses, along with the fact that there was a warrant for his arrest in San Francisco on charges of assaulting his former wife,[85] led to an eight-year sentence. Initially, he was placed in the dreaded U-Boot basement section of Hohenschönhausen prison[86], the windowless, dank, bunker-like basement section of the prison known for torture tactics. He served the rest of his sentence at Bautzen II, the same prison where van Altena had spent many months.

For a year-and-a-half, Lovett worked at an assembly line in a factory near Bauzen II prison. At a press conference following his release, Lovett stated that "he was beaten, and was treated like a spy,"[87] although specifications were never given. He was released on 3 February 1967, together with three other Americans, but his freedom was short lived. Three days after his release, he was arrested in West Berlin. "Mr. Lovett, 26 years old, was wanted on fraud charges by the police in West Germany and Sweden", the spokesman said.

On 19 September 1965, only four months after William Lovett's arrest, two Americans were captured while trying to help East Germans flee to West Berlin. Frederick Matthews, age 22, and Moses Herrin, age 24, were both ex-GIs living in West Berlin after their Army tours had ended. Herrin, originally from Akron, Ohio, later recalled: "I was in my early 20s, naive, one day Fred [Matthews] came and said 'Hey man, I got a deal. They want us to take a passport to East Germany and help someone get out.' So, we talked to a German guy, who was a front for this organization, that was doing the rescue or smuggling or whatever you want to call it. ... Later on, I found out this organization had the OK of the West German government and the CIA."[88] Herrin and Matthews agreed to smuggle East Germans into West Berlin in exchange for money.

Herrin was a fluent German speaker and an interpreter at the US base. Matthews, originally from Ellwood, Pennsylvania, also a German speaker, wanted to start a business in West Berlin. Both men were idealistic, adventurous, and eager to earn money. "As far as I know, Fred [Matthews] and I are the only American Negroes who've been involved in the dangerous game of *Fluchthilfe* — of trying to outsmart the bullets and mine fields, the electronic warning devices, and the sharp-eyed Vopos [guards] in order to give freedom to a few of those caught on the wrong side of the hated Wall. We got involved in *Fluchthilfe* because we were there in West Berlin, broke, wanting to live the easy life. We had been discharged from the US Army and had decided to settle down in Germany for a while."[89]

They were recruited at a favorite GI hangout in West Berlin, the Sportpalais, by a man who hinted they could make some easy money "if you can keep your mouths shut, play it cool and drive an automobile." They were offered 1,000 Marks, an average monthly wage for a German.[90] Later they found out this man was part of what was called a "Scarlet Pimpernel" ring, an organized agency specially designed to help East Germans escape to the West.

Since only Herrin had a German driver's license, he was given the primary responsibility in the escape plan. The car they were given was an altered Peugeot 404, with a smaller, front-wheel drive engine, leaving the transmission shaft free to accommodate an average person. Herrin and Matthews were to pose as students or tourists in East Berlin, meet a designated contact person at or near Alexanderplatz to receive instructions for pick-up locations, help the escapee into the hiding spot and then "drive casually back through the checkpoint into West Berlin."[91]

They successfully transported five people to freedom, but their luck ran out on 19 September. Their initial inspection at Checkpoint Charlie proceeded normally, but when their passports were checked in the customs shack, a guard approached them and informed them that a detailed search of their Peugeot was necessary. Guards tore apart the car for more than two hours before the terrified 13-year-old girl made a slight noise and revealed her location.

Herrin and Matthews spent the next three months being interrogated at Hohenschönhausen prison. Since they refused to cooperate, both men were subjected to flood lights at 15-minute intervals all night in their cells. As Herrin later commented: "I had read enough to know that this was all a part of their efforts to soften me up for the questioning."[92] Herrin soon found out that the Stasi knew every detail of their escape tactics since one of their East German contacts had revealed all to the Stasi after they had also been arrested. Herrin's interrogator took the friendly approach, trying to use his race as bait, buttering him up by praising jazz and blues music and implying that the color of his skin led him to this predicament. After all, there was no reason to protect the ring leaders of the exfiltration organization, who had taken advantage of Herrin and Matthews. Both men were surprised by the efficiency of the Stasi intelligence service in finding details of their Army carees.

Their trial was scheduled for 21 December in Potsdam rather than Berlin to keep the trial secret. "The Four Power Treaty allows Americans — including newsmen — to move freely in East Berlin. But to leave the city limits, an East German visa is required. No reporters, no American legal advisers, no members of our families would be allowed in Potsdam for the trial."[93] Wolfgang Vogel, their East German lawyer, met them the day before the trial, telling them they would most likely receive a six-year sentence. The prosecutor, however, demanded "the maximum penalty" of eight years of "general labor".

For the first three months, Herrin and Matthews were kept at Lindenstraße 54/55 prison in Potsdam. Herrin expressed his surprise: "We did no work, and except for the steel bars, might have considered ourselves as guests in a pretty well-run hotel. We believe now that the Communists were holding us out as bait to the American government while negotiating either for hard currency or for a prisoner exchange."[94]

In early April 1966, however, Herrin and Matthews were transferred to Bautzen II prison, the same prison where van Altena and Lovett were incarcerated.[95] The two men shared cell 28 on the fourth floor and were the only blacks in the prison. When they arrived and walked down the cell corridor, they overheard a prisoner exclaim: "Look! Look! We're getting black ones, too. Now we have integration in this lovely hotel."

They worked daily eight-hour shifts, assembling electronic instruments used in the coal mines. There they met and befriended William Lovett, their fellow American prisoner. Exercise was restricted to half-hour daily sessions in an outdoor exercise cell. Reading privileges and watching German propaganda films were granted once a week in return for good behavior. Both Herrin and Matthews, however, went on several work strikes to protest the terrible prison food.

In general, though, they received preferential treatment due to their skin color. "The Communists want to impress black people all over the world that they have a special affection for the downtrodden races."[96] Herrin and Matthews decided to take advantage of this view and broke several prison rules (such as conversing with other prisoners), knowing the guards would not punish them. Herrin even claimed to befriend one of the young East German guards, who showed a special interest in all things American.

The many months of imprisonment made the men reflect on their lives. "I began relating my own life — and, actually, the kind of lives that most Negro Americans are forced to live — to the lives of those I had tried to help [escape]. There is a difference, I know, between being hemmed in by the carefully drawn boundary lines of Negro ghetto life in America and being imprisoned by the mine field and 300 miles of barriers that seal East Germany from the free West. But how great is the difference? How great, really, is the crushing of freedom by political prisoners, mine field and machine gun bullets and the denial of freedoms by fire hoses, police dogs and a dynamite bomb on the frame of factory work's pickup truck?"

Race repression and discrimination made Herrin feel compassionate towards the plight of East Germans. His focus was on the idealistic motives, not the rule of law. "In the cell in Bautzen II I came to really know the reason why I had continued going back to East Berlin again and again. I had been hooked when the first escapee, a young and beautiful East German nurse, climbed out of the Peugeot 404 on a quiet street in West Berlin. The joy on her face, the sincerity of her thanks, the tears as she walked away to begin a new life — such things would be, I know, far more important to me than the $125 for each trip I would make."[97]

Around Christmas 1966, Herrin and Matthews were returned to Lindenstraße 54/55 prison in Potsdam. There they met the Washington government lawyer Ricey New, who brought them candy, toiletries, and magazines from the States. New also hinted that they may soon be released. That day came on 3 February 1967, when Herrin and Matthews, along with Lowett and Mary Hellen Battle (another American prisoner), were brought to Wolfgang Vogel's office in East Berlin. There they met Maxwell Rabb, who had worked on their behalf for four months, securing their release.

With great relief, the four Americans traveled in Vogel's Mercedes through the diplomatic crossing point at Invaliden Street Checkpoint. Arriving in West Berlin, "we jumped out, shouted 'Freiheit!', hugged one another and even kissed the ground."[98]

After their release, Matthews settled in Berlin and Herrin moved to Denmark. While Matthews later returned to Ellwood, Pennsylvania, Herrin spend over thirty years living in Denmark, Germany, Holland, Sweden, the Netherlands, and Greece working odd jobs before retiring to his hometown of Akron, Ohio in 1993.[99]

Twenty-four-year-old Mary Hellen Battle, from Oak Ridge, Tennessee, was the fourth American prisoner released on that fateful February day. She was a fluent German speaker and had been living in Germany since 1962 teaching English while studying psychology and theology at the Free University in West Berlin.[100] One evening in April 1965, she met an East German named Rolf Reeh, while waiting for a friend to attend Bertolt Brecht's *Coriolanus* at the Berliner Ensemble in East Berlin. Reeh, a 21-year-old East German soldier, told Battle he was engaged to Barbara, an American from California, and had already served a one-year sentence for attempted escape to join his fiancé in the West. Battle was moved by Reeh's tragic story and sensed that fate had brought them together. Later she recollected that "those soft eyes had silently spoken to me with a sincerity and pleading that I could not ignore."[101]

Battle could not forget Reeh and pledged to assist in plotting his escape. While discussing various options with West German friends, she was warned by a student leader of the Christian Student Movement. "He claimed that there were too many who attempted escape out of purely selfish motives." Battle, however, had a strong conviction of freedom entitlement. "Man can only grow and mature when he exercises his free decision and judgement. Yes. Every man should have the right of choice, the right to decide freely, even if he does make the decision to live selfishly. Man has only one life to live."[102] When legal options had been exhausted for uniting Rolf Reeh with Barbara, tensions between the couple led to a break-up. Barbara asked Battle to deliver a farewell note with money to Reeh and his mother as a good-bye gift.

When Battle went to East Berlin on 24 November 1965, to deliver Barbara's note, Battle first met Reeh at the Haus des Lehrers, where he told her that he had deserted the army. He had been hiding for several days already. Battle realized this move made any escape plan nearly impossible. She wasn't sure how she could help him anymore, but she still wanted to deliver Barbara's letter to Reeh's mother.

While she was at the mother's apartment, Stasi officers suddenly entered the apartment. They demanded to see Battle's papers before asking her to accompany them to MfS headquarters. While she was questioned about Reeh's whereabouts, it didn't take long for the Stasi to accuse Battle of plotting to help him escape to the West.

She was placed in cell 89 at Hohenschönhausen prison, which she shared with Brigitte, an East German who had attempted escape with her fiancé. Battle was charged with helping an East German citizen escape (*Beihilfe der Republikflucht*). The judge proceeded to lecture her: "Even as a foreigner you must respect the laws of other countries. It makes no difference whether you agree with those laws, but when you violate them, you are subject to punishment."[103]

Battle did not adjust well to daily interrogations. Trying to hold back information on escape tactics which she had discussed with Reeh and other East Germans under the constant barrage of questions made her scream hysterically until her interrogator tried a softer, gentler approach. She wrestled with the thought of taking full responsibility for her actions, before finally deciding to confess. As a reward for her honesty, she was allowed to write to her parents. She also received some of her personal belongings from her apartment in Berlin. Her request to change cells was also granted in January 1966.

In March, Battle met Wolfgang Vogel, who became her East German lawyer. Vogel told her that he was working on releasing her and the other Americans held in East Germany. At a later meeting, Vogel revealed that Battle's trial would be in Neubrandenburg during April. She was sentenced to five-and-a-half-years hard labor, but Vogel managed to reduce her sentence to four years.[104] Like van Altena, Lovett, Matthews and Herrin, Battle was sent to Bautzen II, where she assembled small radio parts.[105]

Battle's imprisonment was unusual in that she received several outside visitors. A week after her trial, Jürgen Stange, Vogel's West German counterpart, arrived with Ricey New, the American government lawyer, whom Battle's parents had hired. "When the door swung open, I was impressed with the stately stature of a grand Southern gentleman. When Mr. New spoke in his gentle drawl, he only confirmed my impression. His black, wavy hair was sprinkled with gray at the temples and his face glowed with a smile that could only be American.[106]" He arrived with presents for Battle: a stack of fashion magazines and a bottle of perfume.

A few months later, in July 1966, Vogel and New arrived again, this time with Battle's father. For an American prisoner to have a parental visit was unheard of at that time and had to be kept secret.[107] Her father brought newspaper clippings of Battle's imprisonment, conveying the concern and interest in the West. He also brought her lotions, citrus fruit, chocolate, and instant coffee.

By January 1967, an emissary of the British political activist Lord Bertrand Russell was sent to meet Battle and negotiate with the the East German General Attorney's office (*General Staatsanwaltschaft*) on her behalf.[108] Mr. Colloms, the attorney sent by Lord Russell, informed Battle "that there were two conditions under which I could be released earlier. The first entailed a decision by Walter Ulbricht, President of the Republic, granting remission only after a formal representation had been made to him. ... The other possibility for an earlier release was a remission on recommendation of the Attorney General, showing that the criminal 'had been on good behavior, had shown remorse for commission of the crime, had shown that he recognized the error of his ways, had been rehabilitated and could find his proper position in the society."[109] Battle was eager to pursue these possibilities.

It's unclear whether Colloms consulted with Maxwell Rabb or not, but Battle, along with Herrin, Matthews, and Lovett, was released one month later, on 3 February 1967, through the Invaliden Checkpoint. In all four cases, their sentences had been reduced significantly. After a "cloak-and-dagger" reception in West Berlin, including a press conference where Battle stated she had been treated "like any other German prisoner", Battle returned to the United States.[110] She completed her education, wrote a book of her imprisonment, worked as a counselor to help the underprivileged and called for peace and understanding among religions. She lived in Israel during the late 1970s, advocating for Jewish rights and during the early 1990s lived in Germany with her husband for four years before returning to the United States.

4

Clashes Between an Artistic Quaker and the Stasi

Despite Maxwell Rabb's success in freeing four American prisoners in February 1967, his work was not complete. Another American had been arrested on 7 October 1966 in East Berlin. His name was Peter Feinauer.

The 26-year-old Feinauer had moved to West Berlin with his German-born mother in 1959. He was a student at the Academy of Fine Arts and a taxi driver. His German parents were Quakers and had left their native country at the start of World War II. They set-

Peter Feinauer with his camera, early 1970s. Curtesy Peter Feinauer.

tled in Providence, Rhode Island, where Feinauer was raised. When his father died suddenly in 1959, Feinauer and his mother moved back to her native Berlin. The son inherited his father's technical finesse with cameras, which won him awards for his photographs. He developed a life-long passion for photography and wanted to become a professional artist.

On 7 October 1966, East Germany was celebrating the "Day of the Republic", its national holiday, with a large military parade along Karl-Marx-Allee, from Alexanderplatz to Straussberger-platz. Every year, these military parades spawned protest calls and demonstrations in the West, since the East German military show of force in Berlin went against the Four Powers agreement. In 1966, Feinauer was one of the many spectators watching the parade. He had brought his camera and took pictures of the parade, even though it was against the law to photograph the military and military installations in the East. When a drunken policeman, who was marching in the parade, was beaten nearby, all bystanders, including Feinauer, were taken into custody. Erich Mielke, head of the Ministry for State Security, dressed in his uniform for the parade, gave the order for the arrests.[111]

Ten days later, West German lawyer Jürgen Stange notified the US Mission that Feinauer was being held on espionage charges in a shared cell at Hohenschönhausen prison. Later he was put in solitary confinement without knowing when his trial would take place. "Solitary confinement and the demonstrative omnipotence of the MfS drove even those dissidents who were mentally prepared for the possibility of incarceration to the limits of their strength. On top of breaking down an individual's powers of resistance through forms of 'white torture' came arbitrariness and the degrading conditions of imprisonment."[112]

By mid-April, Stange reported that Feinauer would be charged with three separate offenses: spreading propaganda, collecting intelligence information, and having connections with criminal organizations.[113] His trial, however, was delayed until September, almost a full year after his arrest. Stange speculated that there was a connection between the trial delay and the negative portrayal of the East German regime in the Western press published by former American prisoners. He specifically mentioned Moses Herrin who had published a lengthy article in *Ebony* Magazine in June 1967[114], detailing his own detention experience.

Daily interrogation sessions for Feinauer focused on his affiliation with the artistic community in West Berlin, which was known to harbor informants. He was also questioned extensively about his apparent connection to the CIA. The Stasi thought it was highly suspicious that Feinauer had avoided the draft and refused to believe that it was due to him being a conscientious Quaker objector. Instead, the Stasi considered a collaboration with the CIA to be a far more likely explanation for avoiding the draft. While Feinauer initially refused to answer questions, exasperation and desperation later led him to invent a confession. The constant barrage of questions and accusations wore him down.

He claimed to have met "Hersmann" and later "James", his supposed CIA contacts, to discuss the Leftist movement, and formulate plans for recruiting GDR agents, using his taxi as a rendezvous point for these "conspiratorial" meetings.[115] He supposedly took photographs and film material of border violations and security installations, which were offered to West German and American film companies, including the American broadcasting network NBC.

"He was directed to make contacts in East Germany, sound out the climate of political opinion there, and, if possible, recruit agents."[116] Feinauer claimed to have signed a CIA employment form in October 1961 and continued to work for the agency until his arrest. His story included 32 GDR apparent contacts, including women he supposedly blackmailed to work for the CIA. These women later appeared as witnesses at his trial. Furthermore, he stated that he "participated in two cases of exfiltration involving contact with professional organizers."[117] His accounts were very detailed, and yet they corresponded with Western press reports from the time. Berlin was at the front line of the intelligence battle and border tensions were high following the construction of the Berlin Wall in 1961.

The East-West lawyers, Vogel and Stange, raised doubts about Feinauer's detailed confession. They suggested that Feinauer's mother should visit her son in jail, to see if he would repeat his confession to her face-to-face. Such a meeting was arranged for

1 November, but before then Feinauer was officially sentenced to 15 years imprisonment for espionage on 29 September 1967. "The sentence was the severest ever given a United States citizen by an East German court."[118] Feinauer strongly and vocally objected to his sentencing in court.

Two days later, however, when he met his mother, he told her he had committed the crimes of which he had been accused and said that he deserved his sentence. She thought he would not want to appeal the sentence. While he repeated many of the details that he had told his MfS interrogators, "Mrs. Feinauer got the distinct impression that her son was holding something back from her."[119] With no clear explanation for Feinauer's behavior, US Mission employees speculated that it may have something to do with strained relations between mother and son.

A partial explanation later came from a State Department memorandum, which stated that while Feinauner did not have any direct ties with the CIA, he had produced film material for NBC in 1961 (which was never used by the broadcasting agency). At the time, two US television networks, NBC and CBS, had funded two separate tunnel projects in Berlin in return for the right to film escapes from the East, airing a spectacular prime-time special in 1962.[120]

The State Department memorandum further reported that in 1961, Feinauer "had been picked up in East Berlin by the East German police and interrogated but had been released on conditions that he carry out a minor espionage mission in West Berlin. On his return [to the West], he reported to the American military authorities, who advised him not to return to East Berlin. He agreed with this advice, but apparently went back anyway. There is no indication that he actually performed an espionage mission for any American agency, for the West Germans, or for the East Germans."[121] The State Department concluded that "Feinauer's worst offense would appear to be indiscretion in returning to East Berlin after his first encounter with officialdom there and allowing himself to be found close to a scene of trouble."[122] Furthermore, the case was most likely used as part of a propaganda campaign against the CIA, since the timing of it coincided with the CIA's 20th anniversary. "This occasion may have been seized upon for reminding East Germans of the need to be vigilant against Western intelligence, as well as to exacerbate US relations with other countries."[123]

Whatever the true motives, Feinauer suffered the consequences and was placed into solitary confinement at Hohenschönhausen. At some point, Feinauer believes an attempt was made to poison him so that he would forget everything.[124] As he recalled, while eating one of his meals, he tasted something very bitter which parched his throat and made him ill. After that he refused to eat or even talk. He came close to suffering a nervous breakdown. In fact, Ron Wiedenhoeft, who was in the same prison at that time, overheard Feinauer yelling for help. Soon thereafter, Feinauer was transferred to Waldheim-Thüringen prison, near Chemnitz[125], one of the oldest and largest prisons in East Germany. He spent circa four-to-six weeks there recovering from his ordeal. As part of the recovery therapy, officials even allowed him pen and paper to draw.

By the end of April 1968, there was a break-through in negotiations in Feinauer's case. The American lawyer Maxwell Rabb had worked diligently to secure his release, even attempting to free him together with the other four Americans in February 1967. Feinauer was unaware of such efforts and was never told of Rabb's involvement. Upon his release on 10 May 1968, he was driven to Kreuzberg, where he was met by US Mission staff in West Berlin at the Heinestrasse Checkpoint.[126] After his 19-month imprisonment, Feinauer experienced memory lapses. The Quakers paid for a much-needed rest and rehabilitation stay at the North Sea[127] before he returned to West Berlin where he became an artist and free-lance photographer.

Part Two
Negotiations

5

Maxwell Rabb, the American Attorney

When John van Altena was imprisoned in 1964, efforts to free him were hampered by East Germany's insistence on obtaining a policy change. They wanted diplomatic recognition to be a precursor to negotiations with Washington.[128] Since American officials did not recognize GDR's sovereignty, nor were they willing to encourage any move in that direction, the resulting stalemate forced the State Department to search for alternative options. After exhausting official channels to broker a deal for van Altena, they approached the charismatic Maxwell Rabb who recently had traveled to Leipzig.

Maxwell M. Rabb, late 1960s. Curtesy Rabb family.

Rabb was a former Presidential assistant and secretary to the Cabinet during the Eisenhower Administration who had held several international appointments. He was working as a lawyer in New York City in 1964 when a friend and client, General David Sarnoff of RCA, asked him to visit the 1965 Leipzig Trade Fair. Sarnoff wanted to know which countries participated in the fair and what the US trade potential was.

While a small number of American firms had attended the Leipzig trade fair since the late 1950s, participation remained low since, unlike Great Britain and France, the United States had never signed a trade or cultural treaty with East Germany.[129] The US was recognized as having one of the most restrictive trade policies with the GDR. As a rule, the Americans followed West Germany's policies. Since the erection of the Berlin Wall in August 1961, West German participation at the Leipzig fair had been drastically reduced and was unofficially boycotted.[130] Especially the West German industry abstained from exhibiting at the fair.

A further hindrance for Western firms wishing to conduct business in the Eastern Bloc was the fact that they had to go through the Coordinating Committee for East West Trade Policy (short CoCom), which was headquartered in Paris. The CoCom operated in consent with most Western powers to regulate all technical, military, and economic trade exports to socialist countries. In other words, the CoCom decided which goods could or couldn't be imported to communist nations. Since CoCom placed a limit on imports, it effectively dealt an economic blow to the GDR until well into the 1980s.[131] To offset this revenue deficit, East Germany relied heavily on its annual Leipzig trade fair to attract worldwide business partners. In fact, during the 1960s, more than half of all GDR exports were negotiated at the fair.

The Leipzig trade fair, one of the oldest, internationally recognized trade fairs, was celebrating its 800th anniversary in 1965.[132] Their motto of "cosmopolitan trade and technical progress" was meant to welcome the world and provide an opportunity for self-presentation on an international scale. According to the East German reports a record 735,000 exhibitors from 94 countries participated that year.[133] This twice annual fair (held each spring and fall) was the most important event for trade officials to garner im-

Commemorative medallion from the 1965 Leipzig trade fair, showing the emblem of the fair. Property of author.

port and export deals for the GDR. The trade fair also served as an informal, important discussion platform for politicians from East and West that would otherwise have been difficult to arrange.

To remain internationally competitive, the GDR wanted to establish a partnership in the intellectual-technical fields with their "arch enemy," the United States.[134] There were, however, political concerns in conservative circles in the US that feared that by endorsing the Leipzig trade fair it would lead to "increased respectability" for East Germany.[135]

Since increased respectability was exactly what the GDR had in mind, the East German government drastically increased its lobbying efforts among left-leaning political groups in the US to gain political leverage. It also started an advertising campaign in the United States in the lead-up to the 1965 fair. The East European Trade Enterprise Inc. was founded in New York City by the American communist party in January 1965. Through mass mailings, they wanted to attract American businesses to the fair. Although these efforts were hindered by political agenda and lacking funds, their efforts did have an impact. In March 1965, the head of Du-Pont Germany complained to the American Consul in Düsseldorf: "All DuPont's non-American competitors are showing at Leipzig. … East Germany insists that no contract will be signed with any foreign firm unless they agree to show at Leipzig."[136] West German industry had also decided to end their boycott and participated in the 1965 spring fair, since the 1964 fair "had been less political and more business-oriented than in the past."[137]

Rabb's clients, General David Sarnoff of RCA, and William Rudolf, a steel trading executive, had similar ambitions. They wanted Maxwell Rabb to visit the fair, meet with trade officials and report his findings to the State Department to attempt to invoke a change in policy. Before Rabb could travel, however, he had to present his case to the State Department to obtain a travel visa. Approval was not forthcoming, but Rabb persisted and "with the aid of good friends in high places" was able to obtain entry into East Germany.[138]

Arriving in Leipzig during the spring of 1965, Rabb was astonished at the reception that he received. "What I found was extremely interesting, first of all for my own fascination, I saw the finest caviar and the best of foods given out to all those who were in attendance at the top events. But more important than that, I was entertained by many of the members of the East German hierarchy and cabinet."[139] He met Erich Honecker, Secretary of East Germany's Socialist Unity Party (later Ulbricht's successor as the leader of the country); Willi Stoph, Chairman of the Council of Ministers; East German trade officials, including the minister of trade Julius Balkow; and Gerhard Beil, head of Western European trade; Alexander Schalck-Golodkowski a high ranking politician and trader; Günter Mittag, the economic advisor; and Brigadier General Hans Fruck, the deputy minister of security service and head of security for the Leipzig Trade Fair.

Rabb was amazed at the diversity of goods displayed at the fair and the multitude of countries participating in the fair. The USSR was the biggest trading partner, followed by Czechoslovakia and China, which was exhibiting for the first time in 1965. To Rabb's surprise, West Germany was the fourth largest trading partner, followed by France and then Great Britain. "Now that was a revelation

Meeting between SED Party Secretary Erich Honecker, Minister of Foreign Trade Dr. Gerhard Beil and US Ambassador Francis J. Meehan at the Leipzig Trade Fair, March 1988. Bundesarchiv, 183-1988-0313-123/ Link, Hubert/ CC-BY-SA 3.0.

to me, and I dare say, as it turned out later, for the United States government."[140] Through his high-level discussions and viewing of the exhibitions, Rabb realized the potential of lucrative trading opportunities for the United States. He assured his new East German contacts that he would report his finding to American officials to open transatlantic trade between the two countries.

Rabb's trip started a new East-West exchange. GDR officials invited American business representatives to visit East Germany for meetings with government officials. For example, in 1967, the American industrialist and banker C.S. Eaton Jr. took what was reported to be a "personal trip" to East Germany. During this trip, he met foreign trade officials to discuss building an expanded network of economic contacts.[141] By the end of the 1960s, American exhibitors reportedly had leased the largest exhibition space at the fair. Chemical goods, steel products and machinery were imported from the US, usually through European subsidiaries. Overall numbers, however, remained modest.

Back in Washington, Rabb told State Department officials that "other Western nations were using the fair to sell machinery and other goods to the detriment of American industry."[142] Furthermore, he noted that the East Germans were: "suspicious and hostile towards the West, because they were the seventh largest industrialized nation and yet did not receive official recognition. One gets the feeling that East Germany is still the land of the spy who came in from the cold."[143] His report to the State Department was considered important enough to bring it to the attention of President Lyndon B. Johnson, Secretary of State Dean Rusk, the Assistant Secretary of State for European Affairs William Tyler, and the Deputy Assistant Secretary of State for European Affairs Walter J. Stoessel Jr. (who later served as ambassadors to Poland, the Soviet Union and West Germany). Rabb recalled that the American officials were not only interested in his observations from Leipzig but asked him to maintain contact with the GDR officials he had met.

The American government lifted its trade restrictions with East Germany in June of that year, allowing American businesses to participate in the fall 1965 Leipzig Trade Fair. In addition, the State Department issued visas for Americans wanting to travel to East Germany. As a result, large American firms such as Caterpillar, IBM, General Motors, DuPont, and Honeywell started attending the Leipzig Fair on an annual basis. According to East German records, imports from the United States rose by 273 percent between 1965 and 1966, while exports to the United States also rose by 35 percent.[144] These numbers reflected a growing interest of American companies to conduct business in East Germany.

East Germans also started traveling to the United States in growing numbers. For example, Alexander Schalck-Golodkowski, the East German trade minister for *Kommerzielle Koordinierung* (KoKo), a secret commercial enterprise dedicated to bringing foreign currency into East Germany, spent two weeks in New York City during 1966. He was beginning to realize that foreign trade was imperative — and more powerful than the ideological viewpoint — for the GDR economy.[145] During this visit, he met Maxwell Rabb and Robert B. Anderson, a special advisor for the Bank of America. In his talk with Schalck, Rabb urged the GDR to start a comprehensive marketing and public relations campaign in the US. This would be a way for lobbyists interested in opening trade with the GDR, such as agriculture and chemical industries, to counter the one-sided alliance with West Germany. The East Germans, however, took Rabb's words too literary, overestimating the American government's interest in recognizing East Germany as an important political and economic ally in Europe.[146] In fact, the American government retained a laissez-faire attitude towards GDR trade until the 1970s. Discussing the 1969 Leipzig Trade Fair, the State Department commented: "Private firms are not being encouraged to participate but they will be permitted to do so if they desire."[147]

At the same time, no official GDR trade representation was allowed in the United States. Ultimately, the East German efforts to put a dent in the US-West Germany trade monopoly failed just as much as their efforts to lobby the US government for official recognition during the 1960s. The United States considered its partnership with West Germany infinitely more important than any possible connection to East Germany. The State Department remained leery and assessed GDR's pursuits as follows: "Unceasing efforts to gain recognition from foreign states, organizations, and individuals. The GDR's activities with international organizations of all sorts, its propaganda and its sports, cultural and economic policies are all directed to this all-encompassing end."[148]

A few months after Maxwell Rabb's success in opening trade negotiations with East Germany, he was asked to return to the State Department to discuss the John van Altena's case. The United States Secretary of State Dean Rusk, at the behest of President Lyndon Johnson, personally asked Rabb to initiate negotiations for the release of John van Altena during the late fall of 1965. The State Department was looking for new strategies, and hoped that Rabb's new high-ranking GDR contacts, coupled with his experienced negotiating skills, could free van Altena. The only difficulty was in deciding how to reimburse Rabb for his expenses. State Department officials suggested an affiliation with the CIA, but Rabb declined. He preferred to pay his own expenses and work independently despite the personal risk and uncertainty. In the end, Rabb took a total of 27 trips to East Germany, over a three-year period, on behalf of seven American prisoners, always making his own arrangements and paying his own expenses.

Rabb, who thought "this was a great adventure", wrote a cable to Gerhard Beil, the East German head of Western European trade, whom Rabb had befriended on his first trip to Leipzig. When he arrived at Checkpoint Charlie in West Berlin, he was met by Beil and other East German officials. He was then driven in a car to "a very important government building" for discussions. Rabb later recalled how, right after crossing the checkpoint, he could feel the different atmosphere of East Berlin "that made for a texture feeling entirely different." The feeling caught him off-guard. He noticed in East Berlin what he perceived to be a palatable difference from a "freedom-loving country".[149]

For his initial meeting with government officials, Rabb was taken to a large meeting room with an elevated platform, from which five seated Cabinet-level officials greeted him, including Gerhard Beil, Julius Balkow (East German Trade Minister), Hans Fruck (deputy minister of security service and head of security for the Leipzig Trade Fair), Alexander Schalck-Golodkowski (the East German trade minister for *Kommerzielle Koordinierung* (KoKo) and Heinz Volpert, Mielke's man for special tasks. As Rabb recalled: "That was a pretty hearty welcome, some indication that I must be a person of importance to them. ... They were presenting themselves to me to make certain that I remembered them."[150]

Rabb had traveled with his close friend, William (Bill) Rudolf, a German native, who acted as translator for Rabb. Rudolf was a steel trading executive at Associates Metals and Minerals Trading Executive Corporation in New York. Rudolf recalled how tense this initial meeting was. Julius Balkow, the East German Trade Minister, commenced the meeting by berating Rabb on American policies in Vietnam. After listening for several minutes, Rabb stood up, took his coat, and said: "I've come in good faith as an American to meet with you. I've not come to be assaulted. Good-bye." As Rabb started to leave, Balkow reconsidered, and the meeting finally began properly. Rabb's next ploy was a stroke of genius. He promised nothing while inspiring hope and keeping his opponent on the hook. He remarked: "Gentlemen, I know you want certain things and where I can, I'll help you get them, but you never, ever ask me for anything. It's the worst mistake you can make. You'll force me to walk right out of here and you'll lose any chance of ever getting anything."[151] His ploy worked, since it threw the East Germans off balance and made them want to continue their discussions with him. "That is what Rabb did — he contained problems and compartmentalized them in order to defuse them."[152]

Rabb continued: "I deeply appreciate this opportunity that you have given me to visit with you and to discuss a matter of extreme importance. ... I am here to obtain the release of John van Altena. It would be very good if you will agree to let him go now." He remembered that "the smiles that came on the faces of every one of the people with whom I was conferring was so mocked that I can see it to this day very clearly in my mind's eye." When asked what he could offer in exchange, Rabb replied with an air of indignity, "How could you ask me a question like that, you will get good will. And it will begin a relationship between our two countries." Rabb had stirred up a storm. "They immediately all snapped back at me and the friendly atmosphere evaporated very quickly."

The officials started berating Rabb for all the offenses that Americans had conducted on their soil, including the disrespectful behavior of American soldiers. Rabb replied: "Well, that isn't right, and I know that isn't right."[153] Since he could see that a lot of diplomatic damage had been done, he decided to report back to Washington before proceeding with negotiations. He met with Walter Stoessel, an American diplomat at the State Department, reporting the GDR's concerns. Around the same time, US officials in West Berlin reprimanded an American GI after an embarrassing incident along the Berlin Wall. The timing couldn't have been better for Rabb. He gained credibility from the East Germans, who thought he was behind the reprimand, and prisoner discussions could then proceed. Rabb took three more trips with his friend Bill Rudolf to East Berlin to secure the release of John van Altena. He and Rudolf brainstormed ideas while walking endlessly through the city parks of Berlin, all to avoid being bugged. "I never could learn enough from Max [Rabb]," said his friend Rudolf with admiration.[154]

Later, when the State Department approached Rabb to assist in freeing other American prisoners, he was happy to oblige. "Every time I got close to finishing, they sent me back for a new one." Rabb started traveling with his wife Ruth. This was part of his strategy, to approach them on a personal level. He later recalled: "The fact that I returned with Ruth had a startling effect. It seems to suggest to the East Germans that we were vaulting the diplomatic walk and were interested in them as human beings. This immediately created a more relaxed and friendly atmosphere for the talks that were to follow."[155] Rabb's ready smile, his openness towards others and his engaging personality also helped create a more relaxed atmosphere. The motto he lived by was never to speak badly of anyone, since he believed in the inherent goodness of people. Friends and colleagues referred to Rabb as a truly noble gentleman, a very suave negotiator, someone who could really butter people up."[156]

Rabb made sure time was set aside for sightseeing tours and dinners with his new contacts. He and his wife were treated as honored guests, allowing time for friendships to develop.[157] By 1968, Mr. and Mrs. Rabb had become especially close with Hans Fruck, the deputy minister of security services under Markus Wolf. "For a long time, I observed this small, little, not imposing individual, looking in the back or hanging back with two or three people with him, always sort of following me around at a distance." As they met more often, they got to know each other on a personal level. Fruck was known among his peers for his exuberant energy, his quiet confidence, great sense of humor and supreme conviction of communism. "He knew everything and feared nothing."[158] Despite their different ideologies, Rabb appreciated Fruck's frank nature and down-to-earth mentality. They became such good friends, that Fruck invited Rabb and his wife, as well as their son, Bruce, as honored guests to a sightseeing trip of Dresden.[159]

Although Rabb did not speak German, he never considered that to be a barrier. As part of his strategy of winning over the East German diplomats, he insisted on using their translators to show his trust in them.[160] Rabb felt his new contacts would be less afraid of being manipulated or worried that he would go behind their backs to obtain information illegally, if he relied on their translators.[161] He acted as a trusted friend.

Furthermore, Rabb accepted the fact that East German officials would know all about him and he made it clear that he was working with an open book. Rabb's son, Bruce, also a lawyer in the law firm of Strook & Strook & Lavan, later explained: "They [the East Germans] were overwhelmed, that an American could be so humane and handle negotiations so honestly, casually and most importantly openly."[162] Max Rabb accepted East German laws at face value and acknowledged their reasons for being so suspicious and hostile towards the West. At the same time, he made it clear to them that he was in no position to offer any commitments and that negotiations would be based on a mutual good faith[163]. "To the Communist mind he was the epitome of American Capitalism, self-made, Republican, Establishment, with all its contradictions of service to Civil Rights, War on Poverty, Equal Opportunities."[164] Their respective ideologies could not have differed more and yet that did not hinder discussions.

Rabb knew that the personal approach always works best. "What I did is as old as the hills — the personal private relationship where you break down the barriers. You have to use two styles — never let your country down but always be frank and honest. Instead of fighting over each word for two months, you trust each other."[165] Such a simple and straightforward approach, and yet a tactic that often fails in the complexities and nuances of discussions.

Before leaving Washington, Rabb had asked the State Department what he could offer the East Germans in exchange for releasing John van Altena. He was told they could offer only money, but that had been tried before and failed. Rabb later explained that, while East Germany accepted money from West Germany, "they will not take it from us because they want the Americans to consider them to be above the idea that money will buy anything."[166] Rabb asked the State Department officials how they expected him to succeed if the Americans had nothing to offer in exchange. The Assistant Secretary of State for European Affairs, William Tyler, replied: "We don't expect you to succeed. ... We've got to do it because we have to try everything."[167]

Rabb later explained that, by releasing the American prisoner,

East Germany would help reduce Cold War tensions, helping them to normalize relations between the two countries and ease the way towards improved trade relations.[168] This approach clearly spoke to the East Germans' soft spot. The GDR desperately needed revenue as well as new trading partners. Rabb's strategies worked. After three years of discussions, Maxwell Rabb had managed to free all seven American prisoners. As he later pointed out: "I believe that it is significant that since the first prisoner was freed more than two years ago there has been a reduction of incidents with the United States military [in Berlin] and a palpable increase in trade relations, entirely to our advantage." Furthermore, Rabb stated that the United States had exported oranges, coal, textiles, and some machinery totaling $10 million. "He characterized the sales as 'clearly helping our balance-of-payments problem'.[169]" The East Germans had improved their diplomatic relations with the United States, an important step towards reaching official recognition in 1974.

As a sign of how highly regarded Maxwell Rabb was in the GDR, Rabb later recalled: "The East Germans wanted me to be the first Ambassador. I was not interested, nor did I think it was possible."[170] Rabb considered Senator John Sherman Cooper from Kentucky, who became the first US Ambassador to East Germany, a "first class" choice.

Rabb never wanted to discuss his achievements. While he was actively working on a case, he didn't want to risk compromising the results of his efforts. Afterwards, while he was pleased with the results he had realized, he didn't want to dwell on his merits, feeling it was part of history and time to move on. His wife, Ruth, explained that his work ethic was formed during the Eisenhower administration. "Eisenhower realized that the only way to accomplish something — or bring about real change — was to avoid publicity and work under the radar. Do it quietly to get it done."[171] This became Maxwell Rabb's life motto.

To honor his achievements, Rabb later received a congratulatory letter from Lyndon B. Johnson, after the president's retirement in 1969. "Now that I'm back in civilian life away from the hurly-burly of Washington, I remember with considerable delight some of the good things that were done by our outstanding citizens and yours is one of the most important. Your own efforts in East Germany and

your successes in obtaining the release of the young Americans imprisoned there were outstanding examples of what most gratifies
me about our country and the unselfish good people it produces.
Please know I am grateful as all of your countrymen should be."[172]

6

1964–1965 Diplomatic Chess Pieces

Diplomatic Chess Pieces

Negotiations on behalf of political prisoners held in East German prisons took place within a framework of diplomatic personnel from the United States, East Germany, and West Germany. When Maxwell Rabb was asked to free John van Altena, he worked closely with the State Department in Washington and the American Embassy in Bonn, but his primary contact point was the US Mission in West Berlin.

The Mission held special authority and operated autonomously from the US Embassy in Bonn. As an occupied city, tensions in Berlin often caused trouble for US-GDR relations, and yet these matters were only rarely negotiated directly with the East German government. In fact, American officials differentiated most East German matters on two separate tracks: issues concerning Berlin were discussed with the Soviet Union directly and all matters concerning East Germany were deferred to West Germany.[173] This stance developed out of fierce anti-communism in the United States and from a rather negative public perception of East Germany in the US due in part to a lacking immigrant community in the United States.[174] Since the American government sought a reunited German state, they considered the GDR to be temporal.

When American citizens went missing in East Germany, the first contact point was usually the US Mission in Berlin, working together with the Embassy in Bonn and the Department of State in Washington. These three governmental entities collaborated closely in fulfilling important functions. During the 1960s, Dean Rusk was the US Secretary of State (1961-1969). For Berlin matters, Rusk worked closely with William Tyler (1962-1965) and later John M. Leddy (1965-1969), both serving as Assistant Secretaries of State for European Affairs as well as Emmett B. Ford, Jr, the head of the Office of German Affairs at the Department of State. Another key player was John C. Kornblum, the international relations officer of the Bureau of Economic and Business Affairs at the State Department (1966-1968). Kornblum "devoted a major part of his distinguished diplomatic career to strengthen the alliance between Washington and Bonn."[175] He later became the United States Ambassador to Germany from 1997 to 2001.

Francis J. Meehan, a highly distinguished American diplomat and later ambassador to Czechoslovakia, Poland, and East Germany during the 1980s was another key advisor to Secretary Rusk. He had served as an intelligence specialist in Moscow when the Francis Gary Powers U-2 incident occurred in 1962. Meehan was dispatched by the US Ambassador to the Soviet Union to view the plane wreckage. At that time, he met and befriended the East German lawyer Wolfgang Vogel.[176] Meehan, a fluent German speaker, understood how things worked in Vogel's part of the world and the two men became lifelong friends.[177] When Meehan served as a political advisor at the Mission in Berlin during the late 1960s, he and other Mission officers continued to refer Americans needing legal help to Vogel.

1964-1965 Diplomatic Efforts

News of John van Altena's East Berlin arrest on 10 October 1964, reached the Mission via the West Berlin police reports. The Mission in turn notified the State Department in Washington, the American Embassy in Bonn, and the American Consulate in Hamburg, where van Altena had resided.[178] Family members in Wisconsin were informed that they would be required to hire two lawyers — one in West Germany and another in East Germany to handle the case.

Hiring lawyers in both countries was necessary so that they could act as mediators for the difficult diplomatic discussions between the East and West. Wolfgang Vogel had made himself indispensable for both sides of the German wall "because he provided them with a way of dealing indirectly with each other. He was clearly authorized to negotiate in the name of the Stasi. ... [Vogel] arranged, with considerable elan, the exchange of spies and political prisoners. And he was a superb spy trader, a man as highly regarded in East Berlin and Moscow as he was in Bonn and Washington."[179] He worked closely with the East German State Prosecutor Joseph Streit who provided him with direct information concerning prisoners. Meehan suggested that the van Altena family hire Vogel to defend their son. Surprisingly, Vogel declined "because of difficulties he has experienced with American cases in the past."[180] Later, however, the State officials were told that the GDR had instructed Vogel not to represent van Altena. They were hoping for a "great political offer in exchange for John's [van Altena] liberty."[181]

The family hired Achim van Winterfeld, a Hannover lawyer with close connections to the FRG government. Van Winterfeld in turn suggested working together with the famous East Berlin lawyer Friedrich Karl Kaul[182], assuring the family that Kaul "may be able to bring about van Altena's release, possibly before case comes to trial. Conceivable, payment of 'ransom' by family would be involved."[183] The family took this advice, but the Mission foresaw problems from the start. Kaul had close political connections to the communist SED party and a personal agenda.

> Kaul is used extensively by East German regime for political purposes. At request of West Berlin *Senat*, after [Berlin] Wall, Allies put Kaul on list of undesirable East Germans not permitted entry into West Berlin. In discussing van Altena case with Winterfeld, Kaul mentioned his interest in persuading US authorities to use their influence to have him removed from list of undesirables. It is, therefore, more than likely that Kaul, if retained by van Altena family, would attempt to use case for his own purposes which are not merely private but have political content affecting relationships between Allies and West Berlin *Senat*. In addition, in view [of] Kaul's official status as spokesman of East German regime, it would be undesirable for Mission to establish direct contact with him such as we have had in past with Vogel in other US prisoner cases.[184]

The US Mission believed Kaul saw potential for personal and political gains in the case. It only took a few weeks for that to be confirmed. In early November 1964, van Winterfeld made the offer, he "could say that van Altena would be released immediately if ban on Kaul's entry to West Berlin were lifted."[185] At the time, Kaul was representing an Auschwitz survivor in court proceedings taking place in Frankfurt, West Germany, to which he had to drive by car, since a travel ban prevented him from flying directly to Frankfurt. The possibility of lifting Kaul's entry ban to West Berlin was a hot political issue because of Kaul's notoriety and the complexities of the tripartite alliance governing West Berlin.[186] FDR officials doubted that a direct link could be made between releasing John van Altena in exchange for lifting Kaul's travel ban.[187]

When van Altena's trial was set for 5 January 1965, US officials voiced their frustration.

> Make know[n] to Kaul through van Winterfeld that East German image with American public will suffer greatly as result [of] trial and imprisonment. quote American hardly old enough to know what he was doing unquote. Point out to van Winterfeld that trial scheduled just at time when US govt [sic] under considerable pressure due to US approval license permitting re-export of technical data in connection with construction of synthetic fiber plant in East Germany. No explicit connection should be made between van Altena release and conclusion of negotiations for synthetic fiber plant.[188]

Officials had considered postponing talks between Litwin Engineering Industries of Wichita, Kansas, the synthetic fiber plant mentioned in the telegram, and the GDR but decided that would "overcomplicate our management of an already complicated affair. … It is our judgment that the US interest has been cynically manipulated by Kaul."[189] The Mission shared this frustration, believing that East Germany would not be inclined to offer clemency in the van Altena case.

Fears that Kaul had manipulated the van Altena case were confirmed when van Altena was convicted and sentenced to 8 years of hard labor. Ten days later, on 15 January 1965, Wolfgang Vogel confirmed the Mission's worst fears when he reported that: "he could state positively that Kaul had no authority to make proposal to release van Altena in return for lifting of ban on his entry to West Berlin."[190]

Discussions on releasing van Altena had reached a dead end. While a proposal of adding van Altena to a list of West German political prisoners being ransomed by FRG was considered, nothing seemed promising.[191] The van Altena family, farmers in Milton Junction, Wisconsin, had mortgaged everything to support their son and were becoming frustrated with the lack of progress. While it was not generally the role of the Mission to advise families of prisoners regarding their lawyers, the Mission approached the van Altena family, feeling it was necessary to persuade them to change lawyers. This was a delicate matter that had to be kept secret. They recommended approaching Vogel again, to work in collaboration with Jürgen Stange, which would offer them the best hope of securing a release for their son. "We know of no other immediate alternative to Vogel."[192]

Stange, a West Berlin lawyer, had collaborated with Wolfgang Vogel on numerous prisoner cases since 1962. Vogel and Stange made the perfect team; they trusted each other and formed a lasting friendship in which they counterbalanced each other's strengths. Most importantly, Stange was able to travel unhindered into East Berlin whenever necessary.[193] While West Berliners were generally not allowed to travel to the Eastern Sector, Stange, a resident of Braunschweig with an office in West Berlin, had a travel pass (*Bundespersonalausweis*) which allowed him entry into East Berlin.

By May 1965, Stange and Vogel were hopeful that van Altena could be released in "about ten or twelve weeks" but cautioned that the fact that van Altena had been linked with the "political case of Kaul" made the East Germans consider van Altena a marketable commodity, "whom they should not let go of without obtaining something valuable in return."[194]

Before matters could proceed, however, the Mission was notified that another American citizen had been arrested in East Germany. William Lovett, from San Francisco, California, had caused a traffic accident in Leipzig on 6 May.[195] Lovett had been carrying a loaded pistol at the time and did not have the proper travel papers necessary for visiting the GDR.[196] Vogel became Lovett's attorney.

Only three months later, in August 1965, another American citizen, Benjamin Franklin Whitehill III, was arrested in East Berlin while trying to help an East German citizen escape to the West by lending him his US passport.[197] This latest case differed from the van Altena and Lovett cases; the Whitehill family, from Oklahoma, immediately hired the Washington government lawyer, Ricey S. New, Jr[198] to represent their son. New was authorized "to pay a substantial ransom" to release Whitehill. New collaborated with the East German lawyer, Wolfgang Vogel, on the case.

The Mission cautioned New against using ransom as a negotiation tactic with the GDR. "We have pointed out that if the East has reason to believe that the family is prepared to pay a large sum, they may deliberately handle the case in a dilatory fashion so as to extort the maximum."[199] Whitehill, however, was released 15 days later, after Vogel deliberated on his behalf. Vogel argued that Whitehill was unscrupulously exploited by exfiltration organizers, that he was ignorant of the political situation in Berlin and had operated with idealistic motives.[200]

After the surprisingly quick release of Whitehill, the Mission pressed Vogel to apply a similar tactic in the van Altena case. Vogel, however, replied that the cases held no similarities. Clearly van Altena had planned the escape (constructing the escape compartment in his car); secondly, guilt was established since the would-be-escapees were discovered in the car; and thirdly, van Altena had already been sentenced. Vogel stressed the gross mishandling of the case by the lawyers Kaul and van Winterfeld. Vogel also felt his efforts were being hampered by the fact that Kaul still held a grudge for being dismissed from the case. "Kaul is using his influence with the East German state security apparatus to block a solution to the case now that the family has taken it out of his hands."[201] The van Altena case was a tangled mess.

Frustrated by the lack of progress, the State Department considered a reappraisal of American travel policies in late August. Should the United States continue issuing visas to East Germans wishing to travel to the United States, when the GDR was being uncooperative in releasing American prisoners? Or should US passports be stamped with a warning to American travelers, or perhaps travel into the Soviet Zone should be discouraged altogether? The White-hill case had attracted extensive press coverage in the US as well as congressional interest to the plight of American citizens held by East German authorities. "Public opinion has once more focused on the repressive and 'typically communist behavior' of East German regime. Inevitably, there arises feeling of outrage among Americans that East German communists can indulge in seemingly arbitrary imprisonment of American citizens and at same time various East Germans can travel relatively unhindered in the United States."[202]

Most Americans did not consider John van Altena's actions to be of a criminal nature. Helping people reach freedom was seen as a humanitarian act, even if it went against the rule of law. Frustration was mounting against the hard line that East Germany was taking. In September, a ban of all visas for GDR citizens wishing to travel abroad (with exceptions made for compassionate or emergency cases) was once again debated as was adding a warning in passports to the risk of "arbitrary arrest and imprisonment" for travelers to East Germany. The Mission staff were asked to convey these warnings to Vogel, so that he could inform the East German authorities.[203]

While the Mission shared the same frustrations, they knew the proposed travel measures would not lead to the desired outcome. The GDR "works hard to try to look respectable and such measures would adversely affect its image." Punishing the GDR was unlikely to result in an early release of van Altena and Lovett, nor deter the regime from arresting other Americans in the future."[204]

East Germans wishing to travel to the West had to apply for a visa at the Allied Travel Office in West Berlin. The Allied Travel Office was founded in 1950 by the American, British, and French governments to control the entry of East Germans wishing to travel to NATO countries.[205] GDR citizen had to fill-out paperwork listing travel dates with destinations and a list of possible contacts. They also had to respond to in-person questions before travel papers were granted. Denial of travel visas became an important bargaining chip for the Allied powers in negotiations with the GDR.

During fall 1965, Wolfgang Vogel, the East German lawyer, made an attempt to negotiate a prisoner exchange for John van Altena and William Lovett, but the offer was deemed unacceptable from the American standpoint.[206] State officials worried that prisoner exchanges could lead to a "hostage game," encouraging them "to believe that they could similarly recover other agents in the future by artificially producing a deal through the arrest of US citizens."[207] They suggested instead that Vogel be reminded of the visa refusals. "Suggest you discreetly intimate to him that connection exists between GDR retention US prisoners and above practice."[208]

By the end of September, two additional Americans had been arrested in East Berlin. Moses Herrin and Frederick Matthews, both African American former GIs living in West Berlin, were caught smuggling a girl hidden in their car. Then, two months later, Mary Hellen Battle, from Oak Ridge, Tennessee, was detained in East Berlin on suspicion of helping an GDR Army deserter flee to the West. Like Herrin and Matthews, Battle had been living in West Berlin at the time. Since Battle's father was a member of the US Atomic Energy Commission with high-ranking government connections, his daughter's incarceration generated wide press coverage."[209]

Perhaps due to her father's prominent position, Congressional interest and widespread unfavorable publicity, Battle was granted the special privilege of corresponding with her parents on a monthly basis."[210] Battle had suffered mentally under the constant strain of interrogations. In the eyes of the GDR's penal system Battle's crimes were considered severe, so it came as quite a surprise when after only one month Vogel offered a deal to release Battle. He proposed lifting attorney Kaul's entry ban while also granting Jürgen Stange, Vogel's West German counterpart, permission to practice law in East Berlin. This arrangement would allow Stange to directly represent foreigners imprisoned in the GDR.[211] Including Stange in the deal made the offer more appealing, but the Americans remained leery. After all, a similar offer had been made only a year earlier in connection with the van Altena case to no avail.

By the end of December 1965, the West German Evangelical church also became interested in the Battle case. They discussed: "their willingness to buy Miss Battle out," since she was a theology student in West Berlin. The Mission, however, again was skeptical and thought the church was being overly optimistic in assuming they would be able to free Battle.[212] The East Germans never even acknowledged this proposal.[213]

Around the same time, Vogel presented a far more promising deal affecting both John van Altena and Mary Hellen Battle. He explained that the East Germans were interested in importing steel from the United States and that GDR trade representatives wanted to travel to the United States for trade negotiations. If their visas were granted, van Altena would be released.[214] Using trade interests as a negotiating tool to release a foreign political prisoner had not been tried before, but soon became a major bargaining tool, creating a much-needed break-through in US-GDR discussions.

The man behind this new approach was Maxwell Rabb, the New York attorney whom the State Department had sent to East Berlin to help free American prisoners. Rabb's name first appeared in official correspondence dated 31 December 1965. The telegram states that Rabb met cabinet level officials in mid-December, including Julius Balkow, the minister of trade; Major General Hans Fruck, the deputy minister of security service; and other senior government officials to discuss the American cases.

The GDR was eager to expand commercial interests with the US and wanted improved relations between the two countries. Specifically, Balkow outlined the following priorities: 1) establish better commercial relations with visas granted to GDR businessmen to travel to the US, 2) adopt a more civil process of issuing visas at the Mission Berlin, avoiding a "police station atmosphere", 3) create more respectful behavior by American military personnel traveling through the GDR, and 4) encourage American citizens entering the GDR to "not act in a hostile manner".[215]

Rabb's GDR contacts stressed the importance of creating a positive atmosphere where their country could assert some independence from the Soviet Union. They wanted to establish commercial independence from West Germany and the Soviet Union — and they had money to spend on American goods. Rabb believed that van Altena would be released "on the spot" if the US investigated these concerns and issued visas for three businessmen wishing to travel to the United States. He also stressed that improved relations would result in the release of the remaining American detainees.[216]

Sensing a major break-through in discussions, the State Department agreed to issue the desired visas once John van Altena was released. Regarding the other concerns, they were more guarded.

"We told Rabb we had heard other three GDR complaints many times and investigation had proved them groundless."[217] Mission Berlin concurred. "The prior release of van Altena in return for the granting of visas to Mogk, Steinbach, and Schalck-Golodowski [the three East Germans Rabb had mentioned; Ettlich was the fourth visa request] would in our view be an acceptable price to pay." Mission then asked Vogel about the status of the van Altena case.

He [Vogel] said a curious situation had arisen on the East German side involving differences between the trade and legal ministries. He was not sure what exactly was involved, but the trade ministry had made it known in internal East German discussions that it had developed extremely valuable contacts with authoritative US circles through a 'Senator' with whom it was in contact. Vogel was unable to give any names but said the 'Senator' had seen high officials on the trade side and told them he would be able to arrange visas and important business deals through his contacts in the US government. The result of the 'Senator's' activities, Vogel said, was that the legal side had been pushed aside for the time being while the trade people endeavored to explore the proposals made by the 'Senator'. Vogel added that the GDR trade people had gained the impression from the 'Senator' that his contacts were so good and the US interest in seeing business deals with the GDR go through was so high that no concessions on prisoners would be necessary. In this situation, Vogel commented, there was nothing his contacts on the legal side could do.[218]

The 'Senator' to whom Vogel was referring was none other than attorney Maxwell Rabb. Vogel's description is noteworthy on two accounts; it shows that the trade negotiations were considered more pressing than any legal or political matters concerning the American prisoners and that Vogel, even though he was van Altena's GDR lawyer, had lost control of the case. GDR officials now regarded Rabb as their trade and prisoner negotiator. The Mission's response to this new development was: "His [Rabb's] intervention in the case of the US prisoners has probably led to some confusion and perhaps to differences on the East German official side."[219]

1966 Diplomatic Efforts

As the new year started, American officials were hopeful that Rabb's new approach would bring quick results. "We must attempt to explore every reasonable opportunity to secure the release of these Americans." Even though there were now five Americans detained in East Germany, officials preferred keeping negotiations for van Altena separate from the others.[220]

Wolfgang Vogel approached the Battle family, suggesting that they hire Washington lawyer Ricey New since Vogel wished to "establish New as his US point of contact for use not only in the current cases but also for other future possibilities in the prisoners field.[221]" The Battles concurred and engaged New in mid-January.

Around the same time, Rabb informed the Mission that van Altena would be released "very soon," since the East was interested in improving the atmosphere. There would be no quid pro quo. To maintain the confidence with his Eastern contacts, Rabb hoped for "favorable developments on our side."[222] He stressed the importance of not making the GDR look foolish and thereby endanger future negotiations.

Rabb was known for his empathy and personal communication skills. Former colleagues had noted that Rabb had a way of taking the listener into his confidence to share the problem at hand with a sympathetic understanding.[223] His honesty, integrity and "high code of ethics" also distinguished him, characteristics that the GDR officials came to appreciate.[224] They were satisfied that Rabb's involvement had resulted in the issuance of the requested visas and improved conduct by the American military, items which they regarded "as an indication of good faith on our side."[225]

When John van Altena was released on 16 March 1966 in exchange for the issuance of four business visas, the Mission was eager to brief van Altena as soon as possible to avoid any possible hostile statements against his captors reaching the Western press. Bad publicity could hinder negotiations on behalf of the remaining American prisoners.[226] Additionally, while the West German government was briefed on the successful negotiations, Rabb wanted to avoid publicity at all costs. He preferred issuing a statement stating: "the 'delivery' developed quite naturally in the course of his work as head of the US Committee for Refugees, and that he acted on humanitarian grounds without offering any concessions."[227] American officials concurred and did not issue a public statement of van Altena's release or how it was achieved.[228]

After Rabb's quick success in freeing van Altena within three months of negotiations, the State Department was eager for him to help the remaining American prisoners. While some efforts had been made to free Battle, the East Germans claimed that the Americans showed little interest in Herrin or Matthews.[229] Discussions regarding Lovett were also stagnant, even though there was congressional interest in his case.[230]

Following his release, John van Altena addressed the 1966 annual meeting of the US Committee of Refugees in New York City. Seated to his left is Maxwell Rabb, President of the Committee, and standing to his right is William J. Murphy, Chairman and President of the Americana Corporation, who presented van Altena with a check for his continued law studies and a 30-volume set of the *Encyclopedia Americana*. Vice-President Hubert H. Humphrey, seated next to Murphy, gave the keynote address at the meeting. Curtesy John van Altena.

During April 1966, Wolfgang Vogel was told to "keep out of the Battle case" while Rabb commenced discussions with GDR officials on behalf of Battle, Herrin, Matthews, and Lovett.[231] The fact that Rabb had "more useful channels in the East German government than Vogel" was noted by the State Department.[232]

Meanwhile in the US, Battle continued to generate widespread press attention. Congressmen, senators and even the governor of Tennessee, Buford Ellington, had written letters on her behalf. Then Lord Bertrand Russell in Great Britain became interested in her case after the Battle family approached him. Lord Russell wrote directly to East German Head of State Walter Ulbricht (the Socialist Unity Party Secretary and Chairman of the GDR's State Council), requesting permission for an authorized representative to visit Battle in prison. This visit was organized without notifying her lawyers New, Stange or Vogel.[233] While Lord Russell's representative could offer Battle only moral support, there were other developments in her case.

Vogel announced that Battle's American attorney New would be allowed to visit her in prison. This was unprecedented since no other American lawyer had ever been granted that privilege. It was seen as a great victory for prisoner's rights. "It would be a considerable gain if Vogel's proposal could be realized even on a one-time basis, and more useful if it could be regularized in some way, perhaps on a one-on-one visit basis."[234] New's visit with Battle was scheduled for 28 May 1966.

One month before, on 23 April, Battle was sentenced to four years at Bautzen II prison. The strain of being put in solitary confinement, after sharing a cell for four months at Hohenschönhausen prison, caused her health to deteriorate. Wolfgang Vogel was asked to arrange for her to receive weekly, instead of monthly, family letters to improve her spirits.[235] When Vogel and New visited her in May, New brought her American fashion magazines and told her she would have a cellmate soon.[236] Battle's condition improved.

Vogel tried his best to be helpful. After his failure at securing van Altena's release, he felt sidestepped by Rabb and was eager to showcase his abilities. He approached the East German State Prosecutor's office with the offer of a "general liberalization of US visa issuance in return for releases of US prisoners."[237] No immediate reaction followed.

By the end of June, Vogel reported that Battle once again was feeling down and "asked for books and other materials from her West Berlin room."[238] After this was granted, Vogel went further, suggesting another visit from her American lawyer, Ricey New. This second visit was arranged for 16 July, when New arrived with Battle's father, who brought "American magazines, fruit and cosmetics."[239] Allowing a father to visit his daughter in prison was another unheard-of privilege.

While negotiations for Battle's release continued during the fall, the East German citizen, Rolf Reeh, whom Battle had tried to help, was released to West Germany, after West Germany paid ransom for his release.[240]

During June 1966, Vogel was also busy representing William Lovett at his trial, which took place on 24 June. Lovett was sentenced to 27 months on three charges: deviating from his transit visa, carrying a concealed, loaded weapon, and driving negligently, causing injury to ten people.[241] Wolfgang Vogel petitioned for Lovett's clemency to no avail.

Around Thanksgiving, Ricey New was scheduled for another visit to Bautzen II prison, this time to meet Herrin and Matthews. New wanted to discuss their cases with Vogel and his West German counterpart Jürgen Stange.[242] At that time, the lawyers considered the possibility of releasing Herrin and Matthews in exchange for unblocking a *Deutsche Notenbank* fund so that East Germany could purchase foreign-made computers. The State Department and the US Treasury, however, were against such a deal since they feared a communist Chinese connection with the *Deutsche Notenbank* fund.

GDR officials then proposed releasing the prisoners in exchange for permission to open a trade office in the United States, which was quickly rejected.[243] A possible prisoner swap was also discussed at the time. East Germany wanted Robert Thompson, an American citizen who had been sentenced as a Soviet spy in 1965, to be released "to show other Bloc agents that they will not be abandoned once they are arrested and sentenced." The State Department, however, considered Thompson non-negotiable. "We know of no precedent of exchanging a US citizen convicted of a serious crime for other Americans convicted abroad, for relatively minor offenses."[244]

In early October, another American, Peter Feinauer, was arrested in East Berlin following an altercation at a military parade. Now there were five Americans being held in East German prisons again. While negotiations on their behalf continued, the Americans received an offer in connection with the West German firm J.A. Kahl, one of the largest importers of citrus fruit from the United States. They wanted to expand their fruit sales to East Germany and requested a travel visa for Willy Claussen, their East German General Director of Nutrition.[245]

One month later, Rabb presented another offer. He told government officials that East German trade officials were in favor of having East German goods for the US market stamped "Germany - GDR" to distinguish their goods from West German goods. They wanted recognition of their goods to be on par with West German goods and saw it as a quest for "international standing and respectability." Such an offer, however, would need clearance from West German officials and would provide a greater degree of international standing, independence, and respectability, which went against American policies. A more favorable alternative, from Western perspective, was to follow the British example of marking goods with "Germany (East)", denoting a geographic rather than a political distinction from West Germany.[246] Even though the GDR found this alternate stamp acceptable and contemplated releasing the four American prisoners in exchange for such labeling, the American Embassy halted the proposal over growing concerns that ever greater sweeping concessions were being granted. Would East Germany abuse these gains and possibly imprison more Americans to achieve concessions in increasingly broader areas? Also, would such a move anger the West German Allies?

1967 Diplomatic Efforts

At the start of the new year, after an estimated 400 hours of case work by American officials, Rabb's charm offensive with the East Germans was achieving results again. He had convinced them that the release of American prisoners would give them "good marks in the US papers for letting the prisoners go."[247] Such approval could lead to many favorable outcomes. The settlement consisted of two parts: to facilitate visas for cultural, athletic, business, and scientific purposes and to implement the new import stamp "Germany - (East).[248] The East Germans were willing to release Lovett, Matthews, Herrin, and Battle, but not Feinauer. "The East German standpoint was that Feinauer could not, under East German law, be granted clemency until he had been tried and sentenced."[249]

Late on 3 February 1967, attorneys Rabb and Vogel officiated in bringing Lovett, Matthews, Herrin, and Battle across the border to West Berlin. Notwithstanding the late hour, and to appease his East German contacts, Rabb arranged a press conference late that evening "for maximum US press impact."[250] Despite these efforts, public outcry followed concerning the terms of their release. West German government officials believed the prisoners had been released in exchange for unblocking the *Deutsche Notenbank* account. It is unclear whether the East-West lawyers Vogel and Stange were involved in leaking this false information, but it left the Americans scrambling, having to dispel such notions quickly. They were obliged to publicize that the release terms involved a "general relaxation on non-political visas." Indeed, the Mission granted three visas within a week of the prisoners' release, which fell into the commercial, non-political category.[251]

Rabb's success came as a great relief to American officials. Securing the release of four prisoners at one time was seen by Rabb as "an indication we are making great strides toward a period of greatly lessening tensions in Berlin."[252] He was certain that East Germans wanted to establish normal relations with the United States.

Dean Rusk, the US Secretary of State, personally wrote a congratulatory letter to Rabb, expressing his appreciation. "I have followed with deep interest your efforts to obtain the release of our four young Americans from jail in East Germany and am delighted with their success. Although your part in these events must remain unknown to all but a few people, I know that it must be a source of much satisfaction to you. May I extend my warm appreciation and congratulations.[253]"

With one more American prisoner awaiting justice, Rabb wasted no time. Feinauer's case, however, differed from the other American prisoners since he was accused of espionage, a far more serious crime. Still, in March 1967, only one month after the release of the other four Americans, Rabb approached the Mission with an offer. Gerhard Beil, the East German head of Western European trade and later minister for foreign trade, wanted to visit the headquarters of Phillips Brothers, in the United States, to discuss a possible trade deal. In exchange for his travel visa, Feinauer would be released.[254] With caution, the State Department was willing to consider such an offer only after Feinauer's release. The GDR did not respond.

By early September, the visa-prisoner linkage was still being discussed. There had been no further offers for five months. In frustration, the State Department suggested rescinding four or five visas for East German witnesses in a West German civil case involving Zeiss, the photographic lens manufacterer. "It seems to us paradoxical to issue visas to East German witnesses in order to facilitate US justice in a civil case at a time when the East Germans, by prolonging Feinauer's investigative arrest, are impeding their kind of justice for an American citizen in a 'criminal' case."[255]

Complicating matters more was the arrest of Ronald Wiedenhoeft on 5 September 1967. When his Berlin-born wife, Renate, went to inquire as to her husband's whereabouts, Max Erben, the East German State Prosecutor, told her that the East German law prohibited the release of information prior to formal charges being made. However, he did imply that the charges would be grave. When the Mission contacted Jürgen Stange for details, they received no answer. Stange was preoccupied with mitigating the effect of negative US press coverage from an article that Moses Herrin had published in *Ebony* magazine in June 1967 concerning his imprisonment.[256] After what in their eyes was a generous offer of clemency for the four Americans, the East German officials felt betrayed by the bad press and were unwilling to offer further accommodations.

Attorney Ricey New arrived in Berlin a week after Wiedenhoeft's arrest, to discuss the Feinauer and Wiedenhoeft cases with Vogel and Stange. "Mission officer used the occasion to inform Stange and Vogel that we would be withholding visas in the Zeiss trial and other business cases until the Feinauer and Wiedenhoeft matters have been 'clarified'."[257] Later, however, after consultation with the FRG government, the decision to withhold visas for the trial witnesses was rescinded. West Germany felt it was important to have the East German witnesses testify and advised that refusal of these visas would not pressure the GDR regarding the American prisoners.[258] As a result, visas for the trial witnesses were granted, but others were withheld.

Only a few days later, Feinauer was sentenced to 15 years imprisonment on espionage charges. The severity of the sentence surprised American officials. "The 15-year sentence is unusually severe, the longest received by any US citizen known to have been arrested in East Germany in recent years."[259] What made the case even more unusual was the fact that Vogel and Stange reported that Feinauer had made a full confession to all charges, including inciting propaganda against the State, and helping East Germans escape. Stange claimed that the reason Feinauer hadn't confessed earlier was his "hope that his friends [CIA officials?] would be able to get him out of prison before he was brought to trial."[260] Despite the full confession, there were doubts to its authenticity.

An internal memorandum from the State Department concluded that Feinauer's case was being used by the East Germans as part of their propaganda campaign against the CIA, to coincide with the agency's 20th anniversary. They wanted to warn GDR citizens of the CIA threat and damage American diplomatic efforts with Eastern Bloc nations.

By the end of September, Rabb arrived in Berlin for meetings concerning Feinauer and Wiedenhoeft. He stayed at the Kempinski Hotel in West Berlin but wanted to keep his efforts secret even from Vogel and Stange. If anyone asked, he was on a private business trip. He made little progress on gathering information regarding Wiedenhoeft; his contacts were unwilling to discuss the case. While Stange was unaware of Rabb's efforts at the time, he sensed a change in atmosphere and reported to the Mission that "the Soviets are somehow involved in the Wiedenhoeft case."[261]

Without any concrete information, the US Mission continued its policy of withholding visas. "We strongly recommend that the present ban on business visas for East Germans be maintained until we have some clarification in the Wiedenhoeft case."[262] Rabb's GDR contacts complained about the ongoing visa policy. They felt that the Americans were not holding up their end of the bargain. When the four American prisoners had been released in February, the agreement was to issue non-political visas going forward. Exasperated, the Mission replied that the East Germans "could hardly expect that its release of four unjustly held US citizens would guarantee it a benign US government attitude thereafter no matter what further unjust actions it might take against other US citizens[263]."

Meanwhile, Wisconsin Representative Henry Reuss wrote a letter to the State Department regarding his constituent Ronald Wiedenhoeft[264], requesting that action be taken to release him. The CIA also informed the State Department that "no US intelligence agency had any connection with Wiedenhoeft. So far as we know, he was genuinely in pursuit of the research above mentioned. However, his German name, and the fact that his research subject does sound a little like a cover story, combined with the current anti-CIA campaigns in both the Soviet Union and in East Germany, may have led to his arrest."[265] Undoubtedly, the GDR officials drew comparisons to other art historians like Anthony Blunt, who had confessed to being a Soviet spy three years earlier.[266] There was even a direct connection between Wiedenhoeft and Blunt. They both had close affiliations with the German art historian Rudolf Wittkower.

Tensions at the time were high not only between East and West Germany, but also with the Soviet Union. East Germany felt vulnerable without formal state recognition and resented not being invited to partake in discussions concerning their future. For example, the Soviets had made plans in 1966 to renew their trade agreement with West Germany without involving the East Germans. When the Soviets engaged in a private exchange with West Berlin Mayor Willy Brandt in early 1967, East German Secretary Walter Ulbricht (the Socialist Unity Party Secretary and Chairman of the GDR's State Council) publicly announced fears of an abandoned East Germany.[267] The Americans only added fuel to the fire by sidestepping East Germany as much as possible, dealing only with West Germany on matters concerning East Berlin and the Soviet Union on matters concerning the future of East Germany.

After the end of World War II, the American intelligence community did not have much of a presence in West Europe and yet they were tasked with doing whatever it took to prevent Western European countries from coming under the control of communism. Western Europe had become America's most important platform for gaining access to Soviet and Eastern Bloc intelligence targets. Therefore, the American intelligence community relied heavily on intelligence information from friendly European intelligence and security services.

Starting in 1946, the West German intelligence service (known then as the *Gehlen Org*, later renamed *Bundesnachrichtendienst*) became the leading source for intelligence information on political and military developments concerning East Germany.[268] The Org supplied the manpower, working in collaboration with the CIA, who supplied funding and resources. In the following decades, the control shifted, when the Americans effectively built up their military and civilian intelligence personnel all over Europe, especially in West Germany and West Berlin. "At the height of the Cold War, Berlin was the fulcrum of the American espionage effort against the USSR and its Eastern European allies. As of 1959, there were more than a thousand American spies based in West Berlin collecting information as well as conducting *black* psychological warfare operations aimed at the USSR and its East European allies. The Soviets were so angry about the presence of so many US and other Western spies in West Berlin that they threatened to break off negotiations with Washington over a peaceful resolution to the never-ending conflict over Berlin's future."[269] After the Berlin Wall was built in 1961, the effectiveness of the Western intelligence presence became neutralized and was gradually replaced by more sophisticated means of collecting Soviet Bloc intelligence.

It was within this framework that both Feinauer and Wiedenhoeft were being accused of spying for the CIA in East Berlin. In late December 1967, Washington attorney Ricey New arrived in Berlin to discuss the Feinauer and Wiedenhoeft cases with Vogel and Stange. New wanted to meet with the prisoners, but the East Germans' reaction was one of "adamant rejection" to the idea. New reported that the State Department was very concerned and wanted "to use every available leverage on East Germany to assure just and sympathetic treatment to US citizens visiting East Germany. These cases have aroused considerable public and congressional interest."[270] While official notification on the Wiedenhoeft case was still withheld, numerous articles in American and European newspapers had reported on the arrest.

During New's Berlin visit, Jürgen Stange presented the Mission with two offers. The first came from the Soviets. They wanted to exchange Feinauer and Wiedenhoeft for the Soviet spy Igor Ivanov, who was being held in the United States. The second offer was to release the prisoners in exchange for purchasing IBM computers.[271] While the State Department considered these proposals, they also made it clear no decision would be made until information was forthcoming regarding the two prisoners. GDR officials in turn were exasperated by the pressure placed upon them and the continued restrictive visa policy.[272] Neither side was willing to take the first step and ended 1967 in an impasse.

1968 Diplomatic Efforts

Frustrations continued into the new year. Consideration was given once again to issuing a warning to American travelers entering East Germany. The proposal of trading the Soviet spy Igor Ivanov for the two Americans was fully rejected. "The Attorney General is opposed to any action toward the release of Ivanov at this time. ... There will be no exchange for Ivanov."[273] Providing IBM computers to the GDR was also rejected. With no other viable options, placing increased restrictions on trade and travel for East Germans were the only remaining viable pressure tactics.[274]

In mid-January, when 32 salesmen and technicians from the East German firm Polygraph-Export wanted to travel to Chicago for the *Print 68* Exposition, their visas were withheld pending a resolution to the prisoner situation.[275] This stricter visa policy was extended to almost all East German visa requests, ranging from commercial to cultural categories. Only visas for pensioners and special cases such as UN correspondents were granted by the Mission.[276]

The State Department even contemplated reversing product markings of East German goods imported to the United States, if there was no resolution to the prisoner cases.[277] After Wolfgang Vogel presented these demands to GDR officials, their response was swift and fierce. "I must tell you that these demands were literally described as blackmail by my side. ... As a result of this state of affairs, my side considers the negotiations terminated."[278]

At that point, the American Embassy arranged a meeting with

Pyotr Abrassimov, the Soviet Ambassador to the GDR, to ask for Soviet assistance in resolving the prisoner cases.[279] This approach, however, did not produce the desired results. The Soviets were only interested in having their spy, Igor Ivanov, released, and considered the American prisoners an East German matter. Also, negotiating directly with the Soviets only increased anger of GDR officials, who already felt betrayed by the Americans for withholding so many visas. In their view, the Americans had failed to uphold their promise of facilitating visas after the release of prisoners.

In April, Maxwell Rabb was asked to return to East Berlin for further discussions. While GDR officials wanted to reintroduce a prisoner exchange with Ivanov, Rabb believed that they would be willing to release one of the American prisoners in return for visa issuance for businessmen wishing to participate in the *Print 68* Exhibition in Chicago.[280]

While Rabb met with GDR officials, Soviet Embassy Counselor Victor Beletsky was sent on behalf of Ambassador Abrassimov to visit the US Mission in West Berlin. He reported that the Soviets had investigated both the Feinauer and Wiedenhoeft cases and repeated the official charges against both men. Not only did Beletsky condone the charges, but he also suggested that Feinauer was enjoying many privileges — receiving letters and packages, choosing his own lawyer, and having his mother visit him in prison. Statements regarding Wiedenhoeft were of a similar nature. Most importantly, Beletsy insisted jurisdiction in both cases rested exclusively with East Germany.[281]

Involving the Soviets in the Feinauer and Wiedenhoeft cases, however, did lead to unexpected benefits for both prisoners. Wiedenhoeft was allowed to write his first (and only) letter to his wife and Feinauer was finally able to send a letter to his mother, after eighteen months of incarceration.

At the beginning of May, Rabb arrived in West Berlin for a lengthy meeting with high-ranking trade officials in East Berlin.[282] He specifically requested that Wolfgang Vogel not be informed of the visit. He stated that the East Germans "are by now well aware of the visa policy up and down the line, and it is hurting. They complain that US officials embarrass, pressurize, and harass innocent applicants, through whom there is no hot line leading anywhere."[283] While the trade officials had tried to revisit the Ivanov prisoner exchange proposal as well as the blocked West German fund account, Rabb told them with finality that those offers were off the table. Instead, he suggested that they consider the possibility of a "contrived arrangement to save face on both sides."[284]

Rabb proposed visa issuance for the businessmen attending the *Print 68* Exhibition in Chicago. Additionally, there were businessmen wanting to visit the American chemicals and materials company, Sinclair-Koppers. These visas were considered the most urgent due to their economic importance and time sensitivity. Rabb stressed that this was "an important chance here which is unlikely to return in the foreseeable future." If the visas were granted, he stated: "I am convinced, I am positive, that we will get both prisoners out but at least Wiedenhoeft fairly soon, undoubtedly after I make another trip or two."[285]

While the Mission still wanted clarification on charges against Wiedenhoeft before deciding, Rabb considered such technicalities unimportant in the broader context of the situation. He was focused on the big picture, namely, securing the release of the two remaining prisoners as quickly as possible, while trying to appease the East Germans.

After a second meeting on 3 May, Rabb reported that Feinauer would be freed before Wiedenhoeft. While Feinauer's release was not tied directly to the visa issuance, the Mission agreed to grant the visas in advance of the deliverance on 10 May.[286] When asked why Wiedenhoeft would not be released, Rabb stated that "higher authorities insist that a trial take place." The East Germans also wanted to revisit the Ivanov exchange proposal, to which Rabb gave another firm no.

When the departing American Ambassador George C. McGhee (to West Germany) gave his farewell address in Berlin in early May, the Soviet Ambassador Abrassimov offered a self-styled quid pro quo in the Wiedenhoeft case.[287] He proposed that the United States government take some "gentlemanly steps," in which case he would persuade the East Germans of a possible "expulsion from the GDR in the Wiedenhoeft case." In return, he envisioned allowing two East Germans (a doctor and a professor) to attend the UN General Assembly meeting in New York City. "If these men are issued visas without discrimination, Abrassimov would as a rare exception, arrange with the GDR the release of Wiedenhoeft."[288] Considering the highly unusual nature of this offer, Ambassador McGhee explained why such a proposal was not feasible.

"I pointed out to him that he is relating here two entirely different matters to each other: two US citizens on whom we had seen no evidence to suggest any guilt on the one hand being held in the GDR, and UN matters which involve many others, not only the United States. I also called his attention to the fact that the GDR is not a member of the UN, and that even though the FRG was not a member either, it did belong to specialized UN organizations."[289]

This unorthodox proposal raised many concerns for the American officials. For one, they feared an East German - Soviet coordination in the Wiedenhoeft case. Mission officer Morris stated: "It appears to us that Abrassimov's gambit had basic GDR endorsement and that both sides knew what each was doing on the cases yesterday and earlier."[290] While the Mission felt the issuance of visas to the UN would cause little damage, especially since the visas by themselves would not grant the travelers access to the UN (that would be out of their scope of responsibilities), the American Embassy considered the matter unacceptable.[291]

While officials mulled over these latest developments, Peter Feinauer was released on 10 May 1968. The Mission was eager to avoid any negative press which could hinder Wiedenhoeft's release and told Feinauer to avoid making any public statements which could imperil ongoing negotiations."[292]

At the time, discussions were underway to allow the GDR's former head of Western European trade Gerhard Beil (in 1969 nominated as State Secretary for Foreign Trade) to visit the United States in return for the release of Wiedenhoeft.[293] This proposal had first been proposed in March 1967. While the State Department was inclined to grant this visa, they put a hold on it to test the commitment of the East Germans.[294] There was no need to worry however, since Maxwell Rabb's negotiation efforts progressed rapidly. When Ricey New arrived in Berlin in mid-May, he could sense that something important was transpiring. He wondered if "perhaps some deal [was] being arranged in the background, something we [he and Vogel] know nothing about."[295]

In mid-May, Mission received visa requests for businessmen wishing to visit the US Allied Chemical Plant. The Mission granted the visas without making them dependent on the release of Wiedenhoeft.[296] One day later, the possibility of Wiedenhoeft's release was already being discussed.

Rabb meanwhile had received word from his East German contacts "promising that number two [Wiedenhoeft] will be completed and finished within framework of speediest possible legal limitations." Remarkably, this decision had been reached without waiting for Wiedenhoeft's trial. Releasing a prisoners without a trial had never been done before.[297] When further visa requests reached the Mission from the West German Thyssen Company (partners of Allied Chemical), they came with a warning that they had to be approved or else there would be "very serious" consequences for Wiedenhoeft.[298] In the rush to fulfill this request there arose some confusion over names, but the Mission completed the requests as swiftly as possible to maintain momentum in the Wiedenhoeft case.

All along, Rabb's negotiations were kept top secret. None of the other lawyers — New, Vogel nor Stange — were informed of Rabb's dealings, even though they had all participated in negotiations on behalf of Wiedenhoeft. The lawyers could sense that secret meetings were taking place. This created resentment and eagerness to prove their own worth. On 20 May, Wolfgang Stange visited the Mission to assure officials of his continued readiness "to cooperate with everybody, including Maxwell Rabb," without any "consideration of rivalries and credits in this case." Vogel had reported to Jürgen Stange that "something is going on, Rabb is ever active there, his connections are good in the East as well as in Washington."[299] While Stange and Vogel wanted to prove their continued value to the Americans, they also tried to diminish Ricey New's role, claiming the East Germans disliked New's involvement.

Only days later, preparations were being made for Wiedenhoeft's release on 3 June, a German holiday (Pentecost). Mission wanted to arrange a press conference for the morning of 4 June, prior to Rabb's departure[300] for Bonn, where he was invited to lunch with the new Ambassador Henry Cabot Lodge and his wife, both longtime friends of Rabb. When Ronald Wiedenhoeft was released in the early afternoon of 3 June, Rabb and his attorney son Bruce

Checkpoint Charlie, the Allied crossing point between East and West Berlin, 1965. Photo Gotanero.

met him at the East Berlin Unter den Linden Hotel before entering West Berlin via Checkpoint Charlie.

Wiedenhoeft was the last American prisoner held in East Germany, at least for the time being. His release prompted the State Department and the Mission to review their policies and consider making changes. The restrictive visa policies, which had played such a major leveraging role in securing the release of the prisoners, were to be discontinued.[301] Furthermore, proposals were being made to increase contacts between the United States and East Germany to establish "more normal commercial relations." Officials envisioned unofficial and private exchanges between scholars, scientists, and artists, where American professors in West Berlin could approach faculty members at the Humboldt University in East Berlin. Newspaper editors and publishers could conduct exchanges between American and East German institutions. Finally, a more liberal commercial policy was proposed, with a general licensing policy concerning exports, in the fashion of other East European countries. All these steps were being considered to ease tensions and improve East-West relations. "They might encourage some influential GDR individuals and groups to advocate discreetly and in the right places the adoption of more liberal policies, pointing with professional fingers, and therefore with reasonable safety, at demonstrable advantages."[302]

These optimistic views by American diplomatic personnel for improved relations with the GDR faltered before it even took hold. Only one week after my father's release on 3 June 1968, the GDR announced new passport and visa requirements affecting West Germans wishing to travel to the East. They also imposed restrictions on the movement of freight into and out of West Berlin. West Germans, who had previously only needed to carry identity cards and follow GDR bureaucratic formalities to cross the inter-German border, now had to carry passports with visas issued by the East German authorities, while buses, trucks and barges were charged new transport taxes.[303]

West Germany and the Western Allies responded swiftly. The United States, France and Great Britain denounced the travel restrictions as invalid and "inconsistent with the goal of a relaxation of tension in Europe."[304] They wanted to pressure the Soviets into halting these measures, since the Soviets held the responsibility of guaranteeing free access to West Berlin based on the four-power agreement from 1949. Their protests were also directed at the Soviet Union because the three Western allies did not recognize East Germany's authority in West Berlin and expected the Soviets to intervene.

From GDR perspective, these changes were part of a larger effort by the government, starting in 1967, to use citizenship and international law to pressure West Germany into officially recognizing GDR's sovereignty.[305] In other words, the GDR used citizenship laws to gain international recognition. According to GDR citizenship law, any escaped East German citizen who had become a naturalized West German citizen was still considered a legal GDR citizen. That meant they were still subject to GDR laws and risked being prosecuted if they returned to the GDR. This stipulation remained in place until 1973.[306]

When East Germany announced their new travel restrictions

in June 1968, NATO retaliated by imposing travel restrictions on East German political figures, groups of journalists and parliamentary delegations wishing to travel to the West. NATO thereby canceled any promises that had been made by American officials in exchange for the release of the seven American prisoners. Without any resolution to the conflict, tensions remained high on both sides of the Iron Curtain.

7

Legacies and Resolutions

After his release, Ronald Wiedenhoeft spent the remaining summer months of 1968 living in West Berlin. Our family shared an apartment with my grandparents and my father made preparations to return to Columbia University in New York City in the fall. Wiedenhoeft wanted to enjoy life and be productive after nine months of forced inactivity. "I felt at the time that now that I was free the important thing was to get back to normal life as soon as possible, take up my studies, take up everything where I had left off, not let this affect my life and disrupt everything."[307]

At the same time, his mind was preoccupied. He had trouble sleeping and had a strong urge for movement and fresh air. Early sunrises during the summer months in Berlin prompted him to go on long walks before the city arose. My parents traversed the streets of Berlin, sometimes for three or even more hours. Destinations included Charlottenburg palace, parks, and personal landmarks, including my sister's school bus stop and favorite playgrounds. It was the perfect opportunity for family stories and discussions of future plans- and dreams.

Reflections led to self-discovery. Prior to his arrest, my father had mostly disengaged himself from politics and current events, focusing on family and intellectual pursuits. Nine months of confinement forced him to reassess his priorities. "This experience made me a lot more aware of things, and I must say, regretfully, actually, that I had the attitude that as an art historian I was sort of a non-political animal, and there just isn't such a thing. You just cannot *be* non-political. If you think you're non-political, you're being political in a bad sense. But you should be aware - you should be thinking about things more seriously, and because you think you're engaging in a non-political activity, this is no excuse to *not* get involved in politics."[308] Every citizen had a part to play in making a democracy work, rather than taking things for granted. Simply following the laws did not guarantee safety.

Similar reflections had troubled Mary Hellen Battle. While she believed in following international laws, she felt a higher calling to follow the laws of conscience. "I recognized the necessity to respect the laws of another country, but I also felt that they must be questioned in regard to their interest for humanity. No, to advocate violating laws would be advocating anarchy! I was no advocate of lawlessness. Nevertheless, when personal rights were being denied because of laws, one had to suffer or break the laws."[309] Other prisoners, John van Altena, Frederick Matthews, and Moses Herrin, had felt a similar moral duty to help East Germans escapees. Herrin later remarked on the profound correlation he felt between the plight of East Germans seeking freedom with the Civil Rights violations of African Americans at home. Witnessing the profound thankfulness on the faces of refulgees, he felt compelled to continue to help East Germans escape.

The American prisoners all shared a belief in freedom where the sense of individual rights represented the foundation of democracy. A belief in hard work and service to country equated fulfillment of the American dream. Post-World War II, the US was seen as a beacon of freedom for conquering the destructive powers of Nazism and Fascism in Europe and stopping the spread of Communism. The McCarthyism of the early 1950s only reenforced these nationalistic beliefs, making Americans fear and oppose communism at all costs.

All seven prisoners discussed in this book felt a special affiliation towards West Germany, and West Berlin in particular. With West Berlin as an "outpost of freedom in a Red Sea of tyranny", they shared the belief that "America was a symbol of strength, peace, and freedom in a city surrounded by a Wall that suppressed those very ideals."[310] While their motives and interests for entering East Berlin varied, they shared the belief of freedom over tyranny and capitalism over communism. Ultimately their idealism and lack of cultural understanding brought them conflict with the

GDR regime. My father summarized this dilemma. "I think that this business of trying to be liberal, open-minded and say, well, you know, they're normal over there too; they just have a different system. Let's just try to live with them. To assume that they go from the same set of principles as we do is a mistake."[311]

He later reflected, "my experience has not made me a rabid anti-communist but has reaffirmed my strong feeling against any sort of infringement upon personal freedom." Individual rights had no place in the dogmatic and rigid socialist regime. "The only thing I feel is significant is that in our society although there may be many wrongs that should be corrected, there is a fundamental principle of the rights of the individual. Everyone here takes for granted the fact that you do have individual rights and freedoms despite the fact that people may be wronged or underprivileged, whereas in the socialist states, although there may be theoretically good principles, the rights of the individual in fact are completely subordinated to the ideology."[312]

Wiedenhoeft returned to New York City in early fall 1968 to resume teaching at Columbia University and to write his PhD dissertation on Berlin housing projects from the 1920s. My parents were also focused on building Saskia Ltd., Cultural Documentation, their business of selling art and architecture slides, which they had founded in 1966. Each summer, they produced approximately three- to five thousand slides for sale to universities and museums. Saskia Ltd. was becoming a respected source for high quality original art and architectural photography.

Wiedenhoeft was photographing paintings and sculptures from major European museums as well as architectural monuments throughout Europe. What made Saskia slides so special was a combination of film technology, engineering expertise and art history knowledge. Agfacolor film, the German equivalent of Technicolor and Kodachrome, had been founded in the 1930s. In 1965, Agfa film released color-stable film, meaning the color would not fade to pink or blue over time, which was crucial for accurate depiction.

My father's training as an engineer (BCE, Civil Engineering, Cornell University 1959) allowed him to overcome some of the challenges of working under daylight conditions. Early on, he developed a close working relationship with the Kunsthistorisches

Museum in Vienna, Austria, where officials allowed him to test different lighting conditions with objects behind glass inside cabinets and interior galleries with overhead light. To reproduce the true colors of a painting, he still had to manipulate different lighting conditions. He used multiple lens filter combinations and developed his own film material at Germany's largest film laboratory, the Agfa Lab in Munich.

Securing the permission to photograph in museums was the first step in the process of photographing art works. My father's technical expertise usually impressed museum directors to the extent that they allowed him to photograph their collections in return for a fee and the promise of shared slides for their own collections.

Museum photography most often occurred when the museums were closed, to avoid impacting both visitors and the quality of the photography. A museum guard would accompany my parents (and often us children) into the galleries, where they set up tripods and later sometimes lights. Since the photographs were produced for resale, multiple exposures of each image were necessary. In the early years, 36 exposure films were simply clicked repeatedly through the camera, a task usually relegated to my teenage self. Later, a bulk back was added to the camera, allowing 250 exposures per film roll. The number of exposures taken varied depending on the popularity of the works of art and whether it was pictured in major art history textbooks.

My father had a special eye for detail. His knowledge of art history and experience in teaching allowed him to recognize meaningful details that would appeal to professors and researchers. Saskia photographs became known for exquisite details as well as their color accuracy. In architecture, he revealed what the architect had in mind and how it related to its context. In sculpture, he depicted the artist's techniques and the textural qualities of the materials. In painting, he chose details that revealed brushstrokes, symbolisms, hidden self-portraits, or background details. My father considered himself a mediator between dead artists and contemporary art historians.

In September 1969, Wiedenhoeft began teaching at the University of Massachusetts in Amherst. This afforded him the necessary tranquility to finish his dissertation while teaching his favorite subjects in the Art Department for the next five years. He received his PhD in Architectural History with a Minor in Art History from Columbia University in June 1971. Living in Amherst allowed him to interact with other art historians at the five colleges in the area, which resulted in a successful Italian Baroque exhibition. This laid the foundation for an intensive photography campaign in St. Peter's Basilica in the Vatican City during the early 1980s. Wiedenhoeft considered documenting papal sculpture in St. Peter's Basilica his most exciting project. While working in St. Peter's, he was allowed to mount the ninety-foot bronze Baldachin over the first pope's tomb to capture structural details not visible from the ground.

Our family spent three years living in Germany during the mid-1970s, where my father worked on publishing a book on pedestrian and traffic calming measures while serving in a citizen's planning action group. Before a spring 1979 move to Colorado, Wiedenhoeft taught for two years in the School of Architecture at the University of Utah in Salt Lake City.

When Wiedenhoeft was hired as a professor in the Humanities and Social Sciences Department of the Colorado School of Mines in Golden, he found his ideal posting. There he had the freedom to combine his technical engineering background with his intellectual training in art and architectural history. He could consolidate his knowledge to students both in class and at public lectures. Convincingly, and richly documented by his slides, his lectures combined a wide range of disciplines and offered a glimpse into a time and place of long ago.

In conjunction with his teaching career, my parents continued to expand their photography business over the years. The foundation of their business was the premise that original photography in front of the work of art is the only way to capture its true character. They continued to spend the three summer months of every year photographing artwork throughout Europe, and in later years added photo campaigns to Asia.

Adapting to modern technologies, Saskia Ltd. first started digitizing its slide archive during the winter of 1992 with the help of their son Kurt, who provided the necessary computer expertise. These efforts were the first of its kind and received accolades at the

1993 College Art Association conference in Seattle.

In 2004, Saskia Ltd. merged with the newly founded Scholars Resource to create a marketplace of images for a wide group of scholars and image providers. By expanding to offer content from other image providers, the scope and breath of offerings covered more time periods and subject matters. My father's dream of enlightening students to the wonders of art and architecture through high-quality photography had surpassed his wildest expectations. On 28 August 2010, Ron Wiedenhoeft died in Littleton, Colorado, leaving a legacy of beautiful images which continue to be used across multiple continents.

Throughout his lifetime, my father corresponded with Maxwell Rabb, who had secured his release from Hohenschönhausen prison in 1968. Despite their different backgrounds and professional pursuits, they shared common ideals and both men were true humanitarians. Personal correspondence between the two men over a thirty-year time span reveals a shared warmth and support of each other. Rabb revealed that he and Wiedenhoeft had "become good friends.[313]"

Ambassador and Mrs. Rabb with Ronald and Renate Wiedenhoeft at the US Embassy in Rome, 1986. Curtesy Wiedenhoeft family.

Rabb continued to work as an attorney in the law office of Stroock & Stroock & Lavan during the late 1960s and maintained close ties to Washington politics. He had become an asset to both Republicans and Democrats for his liberal views and social activism. He served four US presidents — Eisenhower, Johnson, Nixon, and Reagan — in various official capacities. As a liberal Republican, Rabb believed in broadening the Republican party's electoral base by incorporating New Deal philosophy of solving social problems through government action, legislation, and regulation.[314]

It was while Rabb served as president of the United States Committee for Refugees during the 1960s that he worked on behalf of the seven American prisoners held in East Germany. His efforts in securing their release on his own, without official governmental role, demonstrated his compassion and dedication to humanitarian causes. He thrived at solving tricky diplomatic challenges in unfamiliar circumstances.

While he was negotiating on behalf of the last two American prisoners, Peter Feinauer and Ronald Wiedenhoeft, Rabb was asked by President Lyndon B. Johnson to join the newly formed Commission on Income Maintenance Programs, known as the Heineman Commission. Members were asked to conduct a two-year study, starting in January 1968, to analyze all aspects of existing welfare programs and to make recommendations for constructive improvement.[315] Later, President Johnson nominated Rabb as the US conciliator of the World Bank's International Center for Settlement of Investment Disputes.[316]

Rabb dedicated his life to the public service of the nation. After President Richard Nixon became president in 1969, the President appointed Rabb to an Advisory Panel on South Asian Relief Assistance in 1971-72. The four panel members traveled to Bangladesh in 1972 and reported their finding with recommendations to the President.[317]

In 1980, Rabb became a fundraiser for Ronald Reagan's presidential campaign and an active promoter of the Republican candidate in the Jewish community.[318] After the election, President Reagan appointed Rabb as the US Ambassador to Italy. Despite the usual three-year limit for non-career ambassadors, Rabb retained his post for eight years. He worked on several important projects promoting cooperation between the United States and Italy, including the deployment of intermediate range nuclear weapons in Italy and a new extraction treaty to facilitate joint action in the prosecution of international drug traffickers and organized crime.[319]

Those years in Italy were not without peril. In 1988, an assassination attempt by Libya's Colonel Gadhafi was made on Rabb's life in retaliation for the American downing of two Libyan jets over the Mediterranean Sea. Three years earlier, when the Italian cruise ship *MS Achille Lauro* was hijacked by representatives of the Palestine Liberation Front, the United States had to violate Italian airspace to bring down the plane carrying the perpetrators, destabilizing the Italian government in the process.[320]

In April 1988, Rabb became the longest serving American Ambassador to Italy. To recognize and honor his distinguished diplomatic service, as well as his four decades of public service, the House of Representatives held a special tribute for Maxwell Rabb on 18 April. Peter W. Rodino, the Democratic Congressman from New Jersey and chairman of the House Judiciary Committee, sponsored this special tribute. In a bipartisan effort, nine congressmen spoke on behalf of Rabb's achievements.

Rabb remained active as an attorney in New York City and served on numerous membership boards until the end of his life. He died on 9 June 2002. In addition to family and friends, the Democratic Senators Charles Randell and Patrick Leahy as well as His Eminence Cardinal Edward Egan delivered eulogies at his funeral.

During the 1960s, Maxwell Rabb had laid the groundwork for diplomats negotiating for the release of American prisoners held in East Germany. Offering trade opportunities became an important bargaining tool in addition to granting travel visas.

At the same time, West German politics continued to play an important role in East-West negotiations, with the United States deferring to its West German ally. The Hallstein Doctrine, from 1955, stipulated that West Germany had the exclusive right to represent all German states and that the government would avoid diplomatic relations with countries (except the Soviet Union) that recognized the GDR.[321] A change to that approach came in 1969 with the *Ostpolitik* (Eastern policy) of Chancellor Willy Brandt. To ease tensions, Brandt agreed to negotiate with the Communist Bloc. The Treaty of Moscow was signed in August 1970 by representatives of West Germany and the Soviet Union to lay the groundwork for a Cold War détente, thereby strengthening peace and security in Europe and around the world. Article III of that treaty stipulated that the frontier of all European states was inviolable, including the frontier between West and East Germany. In doing so, the GDR gained de facto recognition, bringing it closer to sovereignty.

Following the ratification of other treaties with Eastern Bloc countries during the early 1970s, a Quadripartite Agreement was signed by ambassadors of the Allied powers in September 1971 and implemented in June 1972. This agreement addressed the status of Berlin, acknowledging the city's ties to West Germany (although not formally recognizing it as West German territory). It guaranteed improved transit to and from West Berlin and eased travel restrictions for West Berliners visiting the GDR. Increased contacts between West and East led to a growing Westernization of values in the GDR during the 1970s. These societal changes were tolerated by the East German state in exchange for "the flow of hard currency in the form of increased foreign trade, loans, and monetary payments from the Federal Republic."[322]

The Quadripartite Agreement gave the GDR the international recognition it had sought by having the name of its state, the German Democratic Republic, appear for the first time in an official document. East and West Germany pledged to respect one another's sovereignty, exchange diplomatic missions, and develop commercial and cultural exchanges. They also agreed to establish tourism and communications relations. Following this agreement, both German states became full members of the United Nations in June 1973.

After 25 years, the German Democratic Republic had achieved what it had sought all along. From the American standpoint however, official recognition did not affect policy changes or a new outlook towards the communist state. The US continued to view the GDR as a subservient satellite state to the Soviet Union, offering few incentives for an improved relationship. Very few American citizens lived in East Germany and there was no significant East German immigrant population in the US. Additionally, the GDR offered minimal economic incentive and American investment in the GDRs national economy remained almost nonexistent. Even the participation of American firms at the annual Leipzig Trade Fair never amounted to much.[323]

The United States was one of the last NATO member states to open its East German embassy in September 1974, in addition to a cultural center in the capital but plans for additional US consulates in other cities were never realized. The US relationship with the GDR continued to reflect that of its relationship with the Soviet Union. Until reunification in 1989, the two countries remained at an impasse.

Paranoia had dictated the rigid ideology of the GDR. It was this paranoia that caused repeated conflicts with the West, imprisoned idealistic Americans, and prevented the regime from gaining improved relations with the US. Some prisoners, like Mary Hellen Battle and Ronald Wiedenhoeft, had tried to reason with their captors but learned that the communist dogma was too ingrained and allowed no flexibility. Maxwell Rabb, the seasoned diplomat, had recognized these limitations and ensured that his diplomatic efforts offered mutually beneficial solutions to appease both sides. The GDR regime never achieved the goal of better relations with its "enemy", the United States, precisely because of its oppressive ideology. Until reunification with West Germany in 1990, East Germany remained stigmatized as the Wall State.

Notes

1. Beil, Gerhard. *Außenhandel und Politik — Ein Minister erinnert sich,* (Berlin: edition Ost im Verlag Das Neue Berlin), 2010, p. 18-19.

2. Beil, Gerhard. *Außenhandel und Politik — Ein Minister erinnert sich,* (Berlin: edition Ost im Verlag Das Neue Berlin), 2010, p. 38.

3. Murphy, David E., Kondrashev, Sergei A., and Bailey, George. *Battle Ground Berlin — CIA vs KGB in the Cold War,* (New Haven: Yale University Press, 1997), p. 178.

4. Office of the Historian, Department of State, "The East German Uprising, 1953," https://history.state.gov/milestones/1953-1960/east-german-uprising (accessed 27 May 2021).

5. Murphy, David E., Kondrashev, Sergei A., and Bailey, George. *Battle Ground Berlin — CIA vs KGB in the Cold War,* (New Haven: Yale University Press, 1997), p. 181.

6. Murphy, David E., Kondrashev, Sergei A., and Bailey, George. *Battle Ground Berlin — CIA vs KGB in the Cold War,* (New Haven: Yale University Press, 1997), p. 306.

7. Murphy, David E., Kondrashev, Sergei A., and Bailey, George. *Battle Ground Berlin - CIA vs KGB in the Cold War,* (New Haven: Yale University Press, 1997), p. 307.

8. John F. Kennedy's report to the Nation — Berlin Crisis, 25 July 1961. https://www.jfklibrary.org/asset-viewer/archives/TNC/TNC-258/TNC-258. (accessed 14 October 2020).

9. Carter, Dr. Donald A, "The US Military Response to the 1960-1962 Berlin Crisis," The US Army Center of Military History, p. 4. https://www.archives.gov/files/research/foreign-policy/cold-war/1961-berlin-crisis/overview/us-military-response.pdf (accessed 15 October 2020).

10. "Berlin Crisis," US Department of State Archive, htpps://2001-2009.state.gov/r/ap/ho/time/cwr/17378.htm (accessed 12 October 2020).

11. Carter, Dr. Donald A, "The US Military Response to the 1960-1962 Berlin Crisis," The US Army Center of Military History, p. 7. https://www.archives.gov/files/research/foreign-policy/cold-war/1961-berlin-crisis/overview/us-military-response.pdf (accessed 15 October 2020).

12. "Reds' Prisoner Tells of Ordeal," *Milwaukee Sentinel* (Milwaukee, WI), 5 June 1968.

13. Zusammenstellung der Aussagen des Wiedenhoeft, Ronald bezüglich des Verkaufs von Farbdias, 28 Feb 1968, Ermittlungsverfahren Nr. XV 1777/70, Band VIII, 2629, BStU 000144, BStU, Berlin.

14. Vernehmungsprotokoll des Beschuldigten, 11 September 1967, Gerichtsakte, Band I, BStU 000244, BStU, Berlin.

15. Vernehmungsprotokoll des Beschuldigten, 11 September 1967, Gerichtsakte, Band I, BStU 000246, BStU, Berlin.

16. "Preceptor Recalls Imprisonment," *Columbia Daily Spectator* (New York, NY), 30 October 1968.

17. Wiedenhoeft marked the Berlin map coordinates as 4334, 4338, 4145 and 4442.

On 7 September 1967, the Stasi concluded that these numbers corresponded to the following telephone numbers: 4334 - private line of a US citizen (name crossed out in the records), and formerly the number for the Canadian Military Mission; 4338 - private line for a US citizen (name crossed out in the records), but suspected of being a CIA operative 4145 - nothing listed for this number in the report; 4442 - phone line for the British Secret Service in West Berlin; Hauptabteilung II/7 Überprüfungsergebnis, 7 September 1967, Ermittlungsverfahren Nr. XV 1777/70, Band VIII, 353, BStU 000439, BStU, Berlin.

On 14 September 1967 another Stasi report written by Lieutenant Knospe concluded that the numbers referred to map coordinates, which had been used in West Berlin for a number of years. East Berlin maps were labeled with 3-digit numbers, instead of 4-digits, which may have led to the initial confusion. Hauptabteilung II/7 Überprüfungsergebnis, 7 September 1967, Ermittlungsverfahren Nr. XV 1777/70, Band VIII, 366, BStU 000459, BStU, Berlin.

18. "Preceptor Recalls Imprisonment," *Columbia Daily Spectator*.

19. Transcript from tape recording of Ron Wiedenhoeft's interview for *Look Magazine*, September 1968 (author's family papers).

20. Transcript from tape recording of Ron Wiedenhoeft's interview for *Look Magazine*, September 1968.

21. Bericht über die Zuführung eines USA Bürgers zum MfS, 6 September, 1967, Ermittlungsverfahren, Band I, BStU 00028, BStU, Berlin

22. "Preceptor Recalls Imprisonment," *Columbia Daily Spectator*.

23. "Preceptor Recalls Imprisonment," *Columbia Daily Spectator*.

24. Transcript from tape recording of Ron Wiedenhoeft's interview for *Look Magazine*, September 1968.

25. John Van Altena Jr, *A Guest of the State* (Chicago: Henry Regnery Company, 1967), 43.

26. "Preceptor Recalls Imprisonment," *Columbia Daily Spectator*.

27. Transcript from tape recording of Ron Wiedenhoeft's interview for *Look Magazine*, September 1968.

28. "US Seeking Status of Red Held Teacher," *Milwaukee Sentinel* (Milwaukee, WI), 14 September 1967.

29. "East Germans Charge Milwaukee as Spy," *Milwaukee Journal* (Milwaukee, WI), 14 November 1967.

30. "East Germans Arrest Columbia U Teacher," *The New York Times* (New York, NY), September 14, 1967.

31. "US Denounces Detention of 2," *Washington Post* (Washington, DC), 6 October 1967.

32. Roger Engelmann, "The State Security and Criminal Justice", *State Security — A Reader on the GDR Secret Police* (Berlin: BStU, 2015), p. 113.

33. Süß, Walter, "The Socialist Unity Party (SED) and the Stasi: A Complex Relationship", *Bulletin of the German Historical Institute* 9 (2014): 95.

34. Gieseke, Jens. *The History of the Stasi — East Germany's Secret Police, 1945-1990,* (New York, NY: Berghahn, 2014), p. 37.

35. Spiekermann, Uwe, "The Stasi as Both a Point of Reference and Differentiation: Current U.S. Intelligence Activities around the World", *Bulletin of the German Historical Institute* 9 (2014): 12.

36. Jens Gieseke, "What did it mean to be a Chekist?", *State Security — A Reader on the GDR Secret Police* (Berlin: BStU, 2015), p. 33.

37. Helge Heidemeyer, "The Ministry for State Security and Its Relationship to the SED", *State Security — A Reader on the GDR Secret Police* (Berlin: BStU, 2015), p. 17.

38. Daniela Dünkel, The Ministers for State Security", *State Security — A Reader on the GDR Secret Police* (Berlin: BStU, 2015), p. 28.

39. Helge Heidemeyer, "The Ministry for State Security and Its Relationship to the SED", p. 14.

40. Spiekermann, Uwe, "The Stasi as Both a Point of Reference and Differentiation: Current U.S. Intelligence Activities around the World", p. 18.

41. Roger Engelmann, "The State Security and Criminal Justice", *State Security - A Reader on the GDR Secret Police,* p. 116.

42. Information taken from a descriptive information plaque at the Hohenschönhausen prison in Berlin, 2019.

43. Anna Funder, *Stasiland — True Stories from Behind the Berlin Wall* (London: Granta Books, 2003), p. 223.

44. Haftbefehl, September 6, 1967, BStU 000009, Gerichtsakte, Band I, 3071/71, BStU, Berlin.

45. Verfügung, September 6, 1967, BStU 000004, Gerichtsakte, Band I, 3071/71, BStU, Berlin.

46. Bericht des Ministerium für Staatssicherheit Hauptabteilung IX/1, 7 September, 1967, Anlage 1.1, Band I Straftat, BStU Berlin.

47. Handwritten note by Erich Mielke to General Beater written over

Bericht Hauptabteilung II/5, September 6, 1967, Allg. P 1275/69, Band 1A, BStU, Berlin.

48. Cell information: MfS - AS 107/80, Nr. 5941/67, Anlage 3, BStU, Berlin. Personal information regarding cellmates comes from Ron Wiedenhoeft's *Look Magazine* interview of August 1968.

49. John Van Altena Jr, *A Guest of the State* (Chicago: Henry Regnery Company, 1967), 37.

50. Untersuchungsplan des Beschuldigten, Ermittlungsverfahren, XV1777/70, Straftat, Band I, BStU 00077, BStU, Berlin.

51. Hubertus Knabe, *Gefangen in Hohenschönhausen — Stasi-Häflinge berichten* (Berlin: Ullstein Buchverlage GmbH, 2007), p. 13-14.

52. Botsford, Joe, "City Native Tells of His, Reds' Fear," *Milwaukee Sentinel* (Milwaukee, WI), 10 September 1968.

53. Transcript of tape recording of Ron Wiedenhoeft's interview for *Look Magazine*, September 1968 (authors family papers).

54. Hubertus Knabe, *Gefangen in Hohenschönhausen* (Berlin: List Taschenbuch, 2007), p. 13-14.

55. Vermerk, 23 November 1967, Ermittlungsverfahren XV 1777/70, Straftat, Band III, BStU, Berlin.

56. Blunt's personal connections to Wittkower are discussed in the following book.

Miranda Carter, *Anthony Blunt His Lives* (New York: Picador, 2003), p. 140, 210-211, 424.

57. Letter written by Rudolf Wittkower, addressed to President Grayson Kirk of Columbia University, dated 5 October 1967. This letter was forwarded with a letter by Kirk to Walter Ulbricht. Gerichtsakte Band I, BStU 3071/71, BStU, Berlin.

58. Tobias Wunschik, "Prisons in the GDR", *State Security — A Reader on the GDR Secret Police* (Berlin: BStU, 2015), p. 128.

59. In German: Ein gutes Gewissen ist ein sanftes Ruhekissen.

60. Haskel, Peter, "Preceptor Recalls Imprisonment," *Columbia Daily Spectator* (New York), 30 October 1968.

61. "US Citizen is Freed in East Berlin", *International Herald Tribune* (London), 4 June 1968.

62. John Van Altena Jr., *A Guest of the State* (Chicago: Henry Regnery Company, 1967), 5.

63. (Van Altena Jr, 1967, 6-7).

64. Dave Kopek, "Communist Gun Control," 1990. http: davekopel.org (accessed 12 June 2020).

65. Victor Grossman, "How Gun Control Worked in the Old East Germany," March 26, 2018. http: peoplesworld.org (accessed 12 June 2020).

66. (Van Altena Jr, 1967, 46).

67. Christopher Sturdevant, *Cold War Wisconsin* (Charleston, SC: The History Press, 2018), 96.

68. John van Altena, interview by author, 7 February 2021.

69. (Van Altena Jr, 1967, 44).

70. (Van Altena Jr, 1967, 47).

71. (Van Altena Jr, 1967, 49).

72. John van Altena, interview by author, 7 February 2021.

73. (Van Altena Jr, 1967, 74).

74. (Van Altena Jr, 1967, 106).

75. (Van Altena Jr, 1967, 212-213).

76. (Van Altena Jr, 1967, 218).

77. (Van Altena Jr, 1967, 221).

78. (Van Altena Jr, 1967, 231).

79. (Van Altena Jr, 1967, 233).

80. (Van Altena Jr, 1967, 235).

81. (Van Altena Jr, 1967, 235-236).

82. U.S. Committee for Refugees & Immigrants, "World Refugee Survey 1966-67" p. 41, http: refugees.org (accessed March 5, 2019).

83. (Van Altena Jr, 1967, 243-244).

84. "Two Students Freed by East Germans," *The New York Times,* August 29, 1965.

85. "American Held in Berlin," *The New York Times,* February 9, 1967.

86. (Van Altena Jr, 1967, 215).

87. "2 Negroes Denounce East German Jails," *The New York Times*, February 5, 1967.

88. Lillian Thomas, The Digs, *Pittsburgh Post-Gazette*, 22 April 2015, http://www.newsinteractive.post-gazette.com/thedigs/2015/04/22/a-cold-war-tale/. (accessed 10 September 2019).

89. Moses Reese Herrin as told to Charles L. Sanders, "My Conflict with East German Reds," *Ebony Magazine*, June 1967, p. 94. https://www.books.google.com (accessed 11 September 2019).

90. (Sanders, 1967, 96).

91. (Sanders 1967, 98).

92. (Sanders 1967, 98).

93. (Sanders 1967, 100).

94. (Sanders 1967, 101).

95. (Sanders 1967, 101).

96. (Sanders 1967, 102).

97. (Sanders 1967, 102).

98. (Sanders 1967, 103).

99. Lillian Thomas, "A Cold War tale," *Pittsburgh Post-Gazette*, 22 April 2015, "The Digs" section.   https://newsinteractive.post-gazette.com/thedigs/2015/04/22/a-cold-war-tale/ (accessed 10 September 2019).

Mark J. Price, "Caught in Cold War: Akron veteran recalls 1965 capture in East Germany," *Akron Beacon Journal*, 11 November 2022, https://www.beaconjournal.com/story/news/military/veterans/2022/11/11/veteran-moses-herrin-recalls-capture-in-east-germany-during-cold-war/69623271007/ (accessed 12 November 2022).

100. Mary Hellen Battle, *Every Wall Shall Fall* (Old Tappen, NJ: Hewitt House, 1969), 30.

101. (Battle 1969, 31).

102. (Battle 1969, 34).

103. (Battle 1969, 64).

104. (Battle, 1969, 136, 145).

105. Telegram from US Berlin Mission to DS, 18 July 1966, NA RG 59, GRDS, CFPF, 1967-69 Consular Box 264, Folder PS 7-1.

106. (Battle, 1969, 145-146).

107. (Battle, 1969, 182).

108. (Battle, 1969, 290, 297-301).

109. (Battle, 1969, 299-300).

110. "Four Americans Held by East Germans Are Freed in Berlin," *The New York Times*, 4 February 1967.

111. Peter Feinauer, interview by author, 1 August 2019.

112. Gieseke, Jens. *The History of the Stasi: East Germany's Secret Police, 1945-1990.* (New York: Berghahn Books, 2014), p. 140.

113. Telegram from US Mission to DS, 19 April 1967, NA RG 59 GRDS, CFPF, 1967-69 Consular Box 264, Folder PS 7-1.

114. Telegram from US Berlin Mission to DS, 12 September 1967, NA RG 59 GRDS, CFPF, 1967-69 Consular Box 264, Folder PS 7-1.

115. Peter Feinauer, interview by author, 1 August 2019.

116. Telegram from US Berlin Mission to DS, 3 October 1967, NA RG 59, GRDS, CFPF, 1967-69 Consular Box 264, Folder PS 7-1.

117. Telegram from US Berlin Mission to DS, 3 October 1967, NA RG 59, GRDS, CFPF, 1967-69 Consular Box 264, Folder PS 7-1.

118. "East Germans Sentence U.S. Citizen to 15 Years." *New York Times*, 30 September 1967.

119. Telegram from US Mission to DS, 3 November 1967, NA RG 59, GRDS, CFPF 1967-69 Consular Box 264, Folder PS 7-1.

120. Greg Mitchell, *The Tunnels: Escapes Under the Berlin Wall and the Historic Films the JFK White House Tried to Kill* (New York: Crown, 2016), p. 35.

121. DS memorandum by Donald S. Macdonald to Malcolm Toon, 2 November 1967, NA RG 59, GRDS, CFPF, 1967-69 Consular Box 264, Folder PS 7-1.

122. Ibid., p. 2.

123. Ibid, p. 2.

124. Peter Feinauer, interview by author, 1 August 2019. He believed poison was added to his food. His knowledge of chemistry made him recognize the bitter taste. He wanted the Stasi to believe the poison was working, so he lay on the floor and turned-off his vocal cords, so that he couldn't talk anymore.

125. Telegram from US Mission Berlin to US Embassy Bonn, 29 April 1968, NA RG 59, GRDS, CFPF, 1967-69 Consular Box 264, Folder PS 7-1.

126. Telegram from US Berlin Mission to DS, 10 May 1968, NA RG 59, GRDS, CFPF, 1967-69 Consular Box 264, Folder PS 7-1.

127. Telegram from US Berlin Mission to DS, 14 May 1968, NA RG 59, GRDS, CFPF, 1967-69 Consular Box 264, Folder PS 7-1.

128. "Lawyer Relates East German Tie," *New York Times* (New York, NY), 16 June 1968.

129. Uta A. Balbier, Christiane Rösch, "Mehr als eine Fußnote," *Umworbener Klassenfeind — Das Verhältnis zwischen der DDR und den Vereinigten Staaten von Amerika*, (Christoph Links Verlag: Berlin, 2006), p. 12.

130. Airframe from US Embassy Bonn to DS, 14 September 1964, NA RG 59, CFPF, EPA, Box 1513, TP 8 GER E.

131. Beil, Gerhard. *Außenhandel und Politik — Ein Minister erinnert sich,* (Berlin: edition Ost im Verlag Das Neue Berlin, 2010), p. 26-27.

132. Fairs were held in Leipzig as early as 1165. During the 18th century, Leipzig became a trading center for Soviet, Polish, and British goods. It was known as "the marketplace of all Europe". After WWII, East German government used the Leipzig trade fair as a propaganda tool.

133. Beil, p. 50-51.

134. Balbier, Rösch, p. 11.

135. Philip Matthes, "Der Anerkennungslobbyismus der DDR in den USA von 1964 bis 1974, *Umworbener Klassenfeind — Das Verhältnis zwischen der DDR und den Vereinigten Staaten von Amerika*, (Christoph Links Verlag: Berlin, 2006), p. 50.

136. Matthes, p. 50.

137. Airgram from Mission Berlin to DS, 18 September 1964, NA RG 59, CFPF, ETPA, Box 1513, Folder TP 8 Fairs & Exhibitions GER E.

138. Bruce Logan's oral history interview with Maxwell Rabb, 19 February 1996, cassette tape 1, property of author.

139. Bruce Logan's oral history interview with Maxwell Rabb, 19 February 1996.

140. Bruce Logan's oral history interview with Maxwell Rabb, 19 February 1996.

141. Matthes, p. 49.

142. "Lawyer Relates East German Tie," *New York Times* (New York, NY), 16 June 1968.

143. "Amerikas Reisender in Sachen Freiheit" [America's Traveler for Freedom], *Berliner Morgenpost* (Berlin, W. Germany), 21 June 1968.

144. Matthes, p. 49.

145. Alexander Schalck-Golodkowski, *Deutsch-deutsche Erinnerungen* (Rowohlt Taschenbuch Verlag: Hamburg, 2000), p. 90.

146. Matthes, p. 51.

147. DS to Embassy Bonn, POLADS Feb 4 — *Leipzig Fair*, 29 June 1969, NA RG 59, GRDS, CFPF, 1967-69, Box 1470, TP Ger E.

148. US Mission Berlin to DS, East Germany in International Politics, 30 Jan 1968, NA RG 59, GRDS, CFPF, 1967-69, Box 2113, POL Ger E.

149. Bruce Logan's oral history interview with Maxwell Rabb, 19 February 1996.

150. Bruce Logan's oral history interview with Maxwell Rabb, 19 February 1996.

151. Arthur Rowe's Interview transcript of Maxwell Rabb, unknown date. Used as a first draft for a Hollywood movie script, (private property of the Rabb family), p. 10.

152. Ivan A. Zasimczuk, "Maxwell M. Rabb: A Hidden Hand of the Eisenhower Administration in Civil Rights and Race Relations," (Master of Arts Thesis, Kansas State University, 2008), p. 10.

153. Bruce Logan's oral history interview with Maxwell Rabb, 19 February 1996.

154. William Rudolf, speech at Maxwell Rabb's funeral on 12 June 2002, https://www.youtube.com/watch?v=KOxcZiH4V5o (accessed 8 February 2020).

155. "Lawyer Relates East German Tie," *New York Times* (New York, NY), 16 June 1968.

156. His Eminence Cardinal Edward Egan at Maxwell Rabb's funeral at Temple Emanu-El in New York City, June 12, 2002.

Zasimczuk, "Maxwell M. Rabb: A Hidden Hand of the Eisenhower Administration in Civil Rights and Race Relations," p. 35-36.

157. Author's interview with Ruth Rabb and her son Bruce Rabb in New York, 25 November 2019.

158. Schalck-Golodkowski, Alexander. *Deutsch-deutsche Erinnerungen,* (Hamburg: Reinbek, 2001), p. 139.

159. Bruce Logan's oral history interview with Maxwell Rabb, 19 February 1996.

160. Author's interview with Ruth Rabb and her son Bruce Rabb in New York, 25 November 2019.

161. "Amerikas Reisender in Sachen Freiheit" [America's Traveler for Freedom], *Berliner Morgenpost* (Berlin, W. Germany), 21 June 1968.

162. "Er holte sieben US-Bürger aus Zonenhaft" [He helped free seven

US-Citizens from the East Zone], *Die Welt* (Düsseldorf, W. Germany), 21 June 1968.

163. "Lawyer Relates East German Tie," *New York Times* (New York, NY), 16 June 1968.

164. Rowe's Interview transcript of Maxwell Rabb, p. 9.

165. "Max Rabb Shows Negotiating Skill with Reds" *Washington Post* (Washington, DC), 13 June 1968.

166. Bruce Logan's oral history interview with Maxwell Rabb, 19 February 1996.

167. Bruce Logan's oral history interview with Maxwell Rabb, 19 February 1996.

168. "Lawyer Relates East German Tie," *New York Times* (New York, NY), 16 June 1968.

169. "Lawyer Relates East German Tie," *New York Times* (New York, NY), 16 June 1968.

170. Bruce Logan's oral history interview with Maxwell Rabb, 19 February 1996.

171. Bruce H. Logan's interview of Ruth Rabb and family in Macon, GA, 11 June 2008. https://www.youtube.com/watch?v=iMc4TB7uFq8&t=9s (accessed 8 February 2020).

172. Letter from Lyndon B. Johnson to Maxwell M. Rabb, 20 June 1969. Personal property of the Rabb family.

173. Livingston, Robert Gerald. "The Context: America's Relationship with the GDR." Bulletin of the German Historical Institute 52 (Supplement 9 2014): 33-34.

174. Spiekermann, Uwe. "The Stasi and the HV A: Contemporary Research and Contemporary Resonance." *Bulletin of the German Historical Institute* 52 (Supplement 9 2014): 27.

175. Gizenstat, Stuart. *Imperfect Justice: Looted Assets, Stave Labor, and the Unfinished Business of World War II* (New York: Hachette Book Group, 2009), p. 214.

176. Pötzl, Norbert F. *Mission Freiheit Wolfgang Vogel* (Munich: Wilhelm Heyne Verlag, 2014), p. 93, 96.

177. Whitney, Craig R. "Spy Trader," *New York Times Magazine*, 23 May 1993.

178. Telegram from US Berlin Mission to DS, 11 October 1964, NA RG 84, RFSP, CCSF, 1961-1978, Box 46, Entry P 256, Folder POL 29 Arrests, Detention.

179. Craig R. Whitney, "Spy Trader," *New York Times*, 23 May 1993.

180. Telegram from US Berlin Mission to DS, 15 October 1964, NA RG 84, RFSP, CCSF, 1961-1978, Box 46, Entry P 256, Folder POL 29 Arrests, Detention.

181. Letter from Professor Dr. Gerd Rinck to John van Altena Sr, 23 March 1965, NA RG 59, RREG 1952-1972, Box 8, Folder PS 7-1.

182. Friedrich Karl Kaul, born 1906 in Eastern Prussia, studied law in Heidelberg and Berlin. He entered the law profession in Berlin, but because of his Jewish heritage, he was sent to a concentration camp in 1933. In 1937, he was released on the condition that he would leave Germany. He spent the following 8 years in the Americas, 4 of which were spent in various prisons, leading him to become a vehement critic of the United States. After returning to Berlin in 1946, Kaul became a member of the newly founded Socialist Unity Party (SED) and quickly rose in rank to become the head of the legal advisory office of the SED in Berlin. He was granted permission to practice law in all four sectors of Berlin by 1948, which rendered him a real asset to the Eastern authorities. By 1960, Kaul had become a well-known public personality. When one of the greatest Nazi criminals, Adolf Eichmann, was captured and sentenced to stand trial in Israel in 1960, Kaul wanted to use the trial to attack the FRG for supporting Nazi criminals. He arranged travel to Israel for himself to report on the trial proceedings, which was a groundbreaking decision, since the GDR did not have any official relations with Israel and "his proposal envisaged giving a new, global dimension to East Berlin's Cold War propaganda against Bonn" on an international level. Lorena De Vita (2017) Overlapping rivalries: the two Germanys, Israel and the Cold War, Cold War History, 17:4, 351-366, DOI: 10.1080/14682745.2017.1322580. Kaul's participation in the Eichmann trial led to the West German Federal Court banning him from practicing in the West starting in 1961, siting "Kaul's SED membership was contrary to a jurist's impartiality and excluded him from practicing in the West."Rene Wolf "The Undivided Sky: The Holocaust on East & West German Radio in the 1960s" (Palgrave Macmillian UK Publisher, 2010), p. 68.

183. Telegram from US Mission Berlin to DS, 28 October 1964, NA RG 84, RFSP, CCSF, 1961-1978, Box 46, Entry P 256, Folder POL 29 Arrests, Detention.

184. Telegram from US Berlin Mission to DS, 28 October 1964, NA RG 84, RFSP, CCSF, 1961-1978, Box 46, Entry P 256, Folder POL 29 Arrests, Detention.

185. Telegram from US Berlin Mission to DS, 10 November 1964, NA RG 84, RFSP, CCSF, 1961-1978, Box 46, Entry P 256, Folder POL 29 Arrests, Detention.

186. West Berlin Mayor Willy Brandt informed the Allied Commandants that he might request their approval for a few East Berlin lawyers, including Kaul, to practice in West Berlin courts and vice versa. Telegram from US Berlin Mission to DS, 11 November 1964, NA RG 84, RFSP, CCSF, 1961-1978, Box 46, Entry P 256, Folder POL 29 Arrests, Detention.

187. "We would not exclude possibility that Kaul has been stringing Winterfeld along with promises to get van Altena out in return for Kaul's being allowed to enter West Berlin under lawyers' deal, without his (Kaul's) having enough control of case to make good on promises." Telegram from US Berlin Mission to DS, 22 December 1964, NA RG 84, RFSP, CCSF, 1961-1978, Box 48, Entry P 256, Folder POL 29 Arrests, Detention.

188. Telegram from DS to US Berlin Mission, 31 December 1964, NA RG 84, RFSP, CCSF, 1961-1978, Box 46, Entry P 256, Folder POL 29 Arrests, Detention.

189. Telegram from US Embassy Bonn to US Berlin Mission, 31 December 1964, NA RG 84, RFSP, CCSF, 1961-1978, Box 46, Entry P 256, Folder POL 29 Arrests, Detention.

190. Telegram from US Mission Berlin to DS, 16 January 1965, NA RG 84, RFSP, CCSF, 1961-1978, Box 48, Entry P 256, Folder POL 29 Arrests, Detention.

191. Telegram from US Embassy Bonn to US Mission Berlin, 22 January 1965, NA RG 84, RFSP, CCSF, 1961-1978, Box 48, Entry P 256, Folder POL 29 Arrests, Detention.

192. Telegram from US Mission Berlin to DS, 28 April 1965, NA RG 84, RFSP, CCSF, 1961-1978, Box 48, Entry P 256, Folder POL 29 Arrests, Detention.

193. Wölben, Jan Philipp, *Der Häftlingsfreikauf aus der DDR 1962-63 - 1989*, Vol. 38, Wissenschaftliche Reihe des BStU (Göttingen: Vandenhoeck & Ruprecht GmbH & Co., 2014), p. 49, 126.

194. Telegram from US Mission Berlin to DS, 18 May 1965, NA RG 84, RFSP, CCSF, 1961-1978, Box 48, Entry P 256, Folder POL 29 Arrests, Detention.

195. Telegram from US Mission Berlin to DS, 18 May 1965, NA RG 84, RFSP, CCSF, 1961-1978, Box 46, Entry P 256, Folder POL 29 Arrests, Detention.

196. Telegram from US Mission Berlin to DS, 28 May 1965, NA RG 84, RFSP, CCSF, 1961-1978, Box 48, Entry P 256, Folder POL 29 Arrests, Detention.

197. Benjamin Franklin Whitehill III was arrested on 12 August 1965. He had been in West Berlin only a few hours before he was approached by someone asking him to help an East German escape to the West using his passport. Telegram from US Mission Berlin to DS, 14 August 1965, NA RG 84, RFSP, CCSF, 1961-1978, Box 46, Entry P 256, Folder POL 29 Arrests, Detention.

198. Ricey S. New, Jr was a partner at the law firm New, Macukey & George located at 1250 Connecticut Ave, NW, Washington, DC. By November 1965, New had expressed his interest in working on prisoner negotiations with DS. "In my meeting with New, I was impressed by his

eagerness to participate in this case [van Altena]. He talked enthusiastically about his interest in 'this kind of work', and stated several times that Vogel was the kind of man he could work with. For whatever reason, I believe that New will take this or any similar case in cooperation with Vogel, even if he does not find the proceedings particularly lucrative." Letter from Emmett B. Ford, Jr to Francis J. Meehan, 17 November 1965, NA RG 59, GFDS, RRB&EA 1957-68, Box 1, Folder PS 7-1.

199. Telegram from US Mission Berlin to DS, 21 August 1965, NA RG 84, RFSP, CCSF, 1961-1978, Box 46, Entry P 256, Folder POL 29 Arrests, Detention.

200. Telegram from US Mission Berlin to DS, 26 August 1965, NA RG 84, RFSP, CCSF, 1961-1978, Box 46, Entry P 256, Folder POL 29 Arrests, Detention.

201. Telegram from US Mission Berlin to DS, 30 August 1965, NA RG 84, RFSP, CCSF, 1961-1978, Box 46, Entry P 256, Folder POL 29 Arrests, Detention.

202. Telegram from DS to US Mission Berlin, 2 September 1965, NA RG 84, RFSP, CCSF, 1961-1978, Box 48, Entry P 256, Folder POL 29 Arrests, Detention.

203. Telegram from DS to US Mission Berlin, 2 September 1965, NA RG 84, RFSP, CCSF, 1961-1978, Box 48, Entry P 256, Folder POL 29 Arrests, Detention.

204. Telegram from US Mission Berlin to DS, 7 September 1965, NA RG 84, RFSP, CCSF, 1961-1978, Box 48, Entry P 256, Folder POL 29 Arrests, Detention.

205. Beil, p. 28.

206. Wolfgang Vogel was involved in negotiations concerning Peter and Helen Kroger, Soviet agents who were being held prisoner in Great Britain. Vogel suggested that various US and British prisoners in the GDR, including John van Altena, be released in exchange for the Krogers. Telegram from US Mission Berlin to DS, 19 October 1965, NA RG 84, RFSP, CCSF, 1961-1978, Box 48, Entry P 256, Folder POL 29 Arrests, Detention.

207. Telegram from US Mission Berlin to DS, 26 November 1965, NA RG 84, RFSP, CCSF, 1961-1978, Box 48, Entry P 256, Folder POL 29 Arrests, Detention.

208. Telegram from DS to US Mission Berlin, 30 October 1965, NA RG 84, RFSP, CCSF, 1961-1978, Box 48, Entry P 256, Folder POL 29 Arrests, Detention.

209. Telegram from US Mission Berlin to DS, 26 November 1965, NA RG 84, RFSP, CCSF, 1961-1978, Box 46, Entry P 256, Folder POL 29 Arrests, Detention.

210. Telegram from US Mission Berlin to DS, 1 December 1965, NA

RG 84, RFSP, CCSF, 1961-1978, Box 46, Entry P 256, Folder POL 29 Arrests, Detention.

211. Telegram from US Mission Berlin to DS, 15 December 1965, NA RG 59, GRDS, CFPF, 1967-69, Box 264, Folder PS 7-1.

212. Telegram from US Mission Berlin to DS, 29 December 1965, NA RG 59, GRDS, CFPF, 1967-69, Box 264, Folder PS 7-1.

213. Memorandum from DS, July 15, 1966, NA RG 59, GRDS, RREG 1952-1972, Box 8, Folder PS 7-1.

214. There was some confusion over which US steel manufacturer was involved with the deal. Vogel mentioned Bethlehem Steel, but the State Department only knew of a pending deal with Allegheny Steel. Telegram from US Mission Berlin to DS, 10 December 1965, NA RG 84, RFSP, CCSF, 1961-1978, Box 48, Entry P 256, Folder POL 29 Arrests, Detention.

215. Telegram from DS, 3116, 1965, NA RG 84, RFSP, CCSF, 1961-78, Box 48, Folder POL 29 Arrests, Detention.

216. Telegram from DS, 3116, 1965, NA RG 84, RFSP, CCSF, 1961-78, Box 48, Folder POL 29 Arrests, Detention.

217. Telegram from DS, 3116, 1965, NA RG 84, RFSP, CCSF, 1961-78, Box 48, Folder POL 29 Arrests, Detention.

218. Telegram from US Mission Berlin, to DS, 31 December 1965, NA RG 84, RFSP, CCSF, 1961-78, Box 48, Folder POL 29 Arrests, Detention.

219. Telegram from US Mission Berlin, to DS, 31 December 1965, NA RG 84, RFSP, CCSF, 1961-78, Box 48, Folder POL 29 Arrests, Detention.

220. Telegram from DS to US Mission Berlin, 6 January 1966, NA RG 59, GRDS, CFPF, 1967-69, Box 264, Folder PS 7-1.

221. Telegram from US Mission Berlin to DS, 10 January 1966, NA RG 59, GRDS, CFPF, 1967-69, Box 264, Folder PS 7-1.

222. Telegram from US Mission Berlin to DS, 13 January 1966, NA RG 84, RFSP, CCSF, 1961-78, Box 55, Folder POL 29 Arrests, Detention.

223. Sherman Adams, Rabb's former boss during the Eisenhower Administration, made these comments. *Sherman Adams, Firsthand Report: The Story of the Eisenhower Administration* (New York: Harper and Brothers, 1961), 335.

224. White House colleague, Fred Morrow, made this observation of Rabb. E. Frederic Morrow, *Black Man in the White House* (New York: Van Rees Press, 1963), p. 223.

225. Telegram from US Mission Berlin to DS, 13 January 1966, NA RG 84, RFSP, CCSF 1961-78, Box 48, Folder POL 29 Arrests, Detention.

226. Telegram from US Embassy Bonn to Mission Berlin, 18 January 1966, NA RG 84, RFSP, CCSF 1961-78, Box 55, Folder POL 29, Arrests, Detention.

227. Telegram from US Mission Berlin to DS, 13 January 1966, NA RG 84, RFSP, CCSF 1961-78, Box 55, Folder POL 29 Arrests, Detention.

228. Telegram from US Embassy Bonn to Mission Berlin, 18 January 1966, NA RG 84, RFSP, CCSF 961-78, Box 55, Folder POL 29 Arrests, Detention.

229. Telegram from DS to US Mission Berlin, 31 December 1965, NA RG 84, RFSP, CCSF 1961-78, Box 48, Folder POL 29 Arrests, Detention.

230. Telegram from DS to US Mission Berlin, 20 January 1966, NA RG 84, RFSP, CCSF 1961-78, Box 55, Folder POL 29 Arrests, Detention.

231. Memorandum from DS, 18 July 1966, NA RG 59, RREG 1952-1972, Box 8, Folder PS 7-1.

232. Memorandum from Robert G. Shackleton to Robert G. Livingston, 14 October 1966, NA RG 59, RREG 1952-1972, Box 8, Folder PS 7-1.

233. Telegram from US Mission Berlin to DS, 25 January 1966, NA RG 59, GRDS, CFPF 1967-69, Box 264, Folder PS 7-1.

234. Telegram from DS to US Mission Berlin, 26 January 1966, NA RG 84, RFSP, CCSF 1961-78, Box 55, Folder POL 29 Arrests, Detention.

235. Telegram from DS to US Mission Berlin, 26 May 1966, NA RG 59, GRDS, CFPF 1967-69, Box 264, Folder PS 7-1.

236. Telegram from US Mission Berlin to DS, 28 May 1966, NA RG 59, GRDS, CFPF 1967-69, Box 264, Folder PS 7-1.

237. Telegram from US Mission Berlin to DS, 28 May 1966, NA RG 59, GRDS, CFPF 1967-69, Box 264, Folder PS 7-1.

238. Telegram from US Mission Berlin to DS, 27 June 1966, NA RG 59, GRDS, CFPF 1967-69, Box 264, Folder PS 7-1.

239. Telegram from US Mission Berlin to DS, 18 July 1966, NA RG 84, RFSP, CCSF 1961-78, Box 55, Folder POL 29 Arrests, Detention.

240. Telegram from US Mission Berlin to DS, 27 June 1966, NA RG 59, GRDS, CFPF 1967-69, Box 264, Folder PS 7-1.

241. Telegram from US Mission Berlin to DS, 18 July 1966, NA RG 84, RFSP, CCSF 1961-78, Box 55, Folder POL 29 Arrests, Detention.

242. Telegram from US Mission Berlin to DS, 23 November 1966, NA RG 84, RFSP, CCSF 1961-78, Box 55, Folder POL 29 Arrests, Detention.

243. Memorandum from Alfred Puhan, DS, 27 February 1967, NA RG 59, GRDS, RREG 195201972, Box 8, Folder PS 7-1.

244. Memorandum from Benjamin H. Read, Executive Secretary for US Secretary of State Dean Rusk, to Walt W. Rostow, White House, 26 September 1966, NA RG 59, GRDS, CFPF 1967-69, Box 264, Folder PS 7-1.

245. Telegram from American Consulate Hamburg to DS, 20 October 1966, NA RG 84, RFSP, CCSF 1961-78, Box 55, Folder POL 29 Arrests, Detention.

246. Telegram from US Embassy Bonn to DS, 26 November 1966, NA RG 84, RFSP, CCSF 1961-78, Box 55, Folder POL 29 Arrests, Detention.

247. Telegram from US Mission Berlin to DS, 26 January 1967, NA RG 59, GRDS, CFPF 1967-69, Box 264, Folder PS 7-1.

248. Memorandum from Alfred Puhan, DS, 27 February 1967, NA RG 59, GRDS, RREG

249. Telegram from US Mission Berlin to DS, 26 January 1967, NA RG 59, GRDS, CFPF 1967-69, Box 264, Folder PS 7-1.

250. Telegram from US Mission Berlin to DS, 3 February 1967, NA RG 59, GRDS, CFPF 1967-69, Box 264, Folder PS 7-1.

251. Telegram from US Mission Berlin to DS, 8 February 1967, NA RG 59, GRDS, CFPF 1967-69, Box 264, Folder PS 7-1.

252. Homer Bigart, "Lawyer Sees Cut in Berlin Tension," *New York Times* (New York, NY), 12 February 1967.

253. Letter from Dean Rusk to Maxwell Rabb, 28 February 1967, NA RG 59, GRDS, CFPF 1967-69, Box 264, Folder PS 7-1.

254. Letter from the DS to American Embassy Bonn and US Mission Berlin, 13 March 1967, NA RG 59, GRDS, CFPF 1967-69, Box 264, Folder PS 7-1.

255. Telegram from DS to US Mission Berlin, 6 September 1967, NA RG 59, GRDS, CFPF 1967-69, Box 264, Folder PS 7-1.

256. Moses Herrin published a personal account of his GDR arrest and imprisonment in *Ebony Magazine*, appearing in the June 1967 issue.

257. Telegram from DS to US Mission Berlin, 14 September 1967, NA RG 59, GRDS, CFPF 1967-69, Box 264, Folder PS 7-1.

258. Telegram from DS to US Mission Berlin, September 15, 1967, NA RG 59, GRDS, CFPF 1967-69, Box 264, Folder PS 7-1.

259. Telegram from DS to US Mission Berlin, 3 October 1967, NA RG 59, GRDS, CFPF 1967-69, Box 264, Folder PS 7-1.

260. Telegram from DS to US Mission Berlin, 3 October 1967, NA RG 59, GRDS, CFPF 1967-69, Box 264, Folder PS 7-1.

261. Telegram from DS to US Mission Berlin, 28 September 1967, NA RG 59, GRDS, CFPF 1967-69, Box 264, Folder PS 7-1.

262. Telegram from US Mission Berlin to DS, 4 October 1967, NA RG 59, GRDS, CFPF 1967-69, Box 264, Folder PS 7-1.

263. Telegram from DS to US Mission Berlin, 6 September 1967, NA RG 59, GRDS, CFPF 1967-69, Box 264, Folder PS 7-1.

264. Letter from Henry S. Reuss to William Macomber, 13 October 1967, NA RG 59, GRDS, CFPF 1967-69, Box 264, Folder PS 7-1.

265. Memorandum from Donald Macdonald at DS to Malcolm Toon, head of European/ Soviet Affairs office at DS, 2 November 1967, NA RG 59, GRDS, CFPF 1967-69, Box 264, Folder PS 7-1.

266. Carter, Miranda, *Anthony Blunt His Lives* (New York, NY: Picador, 2001), p. 451.

267. CIA Intelligence Memorandum "Strains in Soviet-East German Relations: 1962-1967", 24 February 1967, RSS No. 0019, https://www.cia.gov/library/readingroom/docs/DOC_0000969854.pdf (accessed 26 February 2020).

268. Aid, Matthew M., "It Did Not Begin with Snowden - The Declassified History of American Intelligence Operations in Europe: 1945-2001", Brills Research Collection *U.S. Intelligence on Europe, 1945-1995*, p. 5-6. https://brill.com/fileasset/downloads_products/36813_U.S._Intelligence_on_Europe_background_article.pdf, (accessed 26 February 2020).

269. Aid, Matthew M., "It Did Not Begin with Snowden - The Declassified History of American Intelligence Operations in Europe: 1945-2001".

270. Telegram from the DS to US Embassy London, 14 December 1967, NA RG 59, GRDS, CFPF 1967-69, Box 264, Folder PS 7-1.

271. Telegram from DS to US Mission Berlin, 21 December 1967, NA RG 59, GRDS, CFPF 1967-69, Box 264, Folder PS 7-1.

272. Telegram from DS to US Mission Berlin, 23 December 1967, NA RG 59, GRDS, CFPF 1967-69, Box 264, Folder PS 7-1.

273. Internal Memorandum from DS, 13 January 1968, NA RG 59, GRDS, CFPF 1967-69, Box 264, Folder PS 7-1.

274. Action Memorandum from John M. Leddy to Mr. Katzenbach at DS, 13 January 1968, NA RG 59, GRDS, CFPF, 1967-69, Box 264, Folder PS 7-1.

275. Telegram from DS to US Mission Berlin, 19 January 1968, NA RG 59, GRDS, CFPF 1967-69, Box 264, Folder PS 7-1.

276. Telegram from DS to US Mission Berlin, 24 January 1968, NA RG 59, GRDS, CFPF 1967-69, Box 264, Folder PS 7-1.

277. In February 1967, the US had agreed to label imports from the GDR with the stamp "Germany - (East)" in exchange for the release of four American prisoners: Battle, Lovett, Herrin, and Matthews.

278. Telegram from DS to US Mission Berlin, 9 February 1968, NA RG 59, GRDS, CFPF 1967-69, Box 264, Folder PS 7-1.

279. Telegram from DS to US Embassy Bonn and US Mission Berlin, 14 February 1968, NA RG 59, GRDS, CFPF 1967-69, Box 264, Folder PS 7-1.

280. Telegram from DS to US Embassy Bonn, 19 April 1968, NA RG 59, GRDS, CFPF 1967-69, Box 264, Folder PS 7-1.

281. Telegram from US Mission Berlin to US Embassy Bonn, 24 April 1968, NA RG 59, GRDS, CFPF 1967-69, Box 264, Folder PS 7-1.

282. Telegram from DS to US Mission Berlin, 29 April 1968, NA RG 59, GRDS, CFPF 1967-69, Box 264, Folder PS 7-1.

283. Telegram from US Mission Berlin to DS, 2 May 1968, NA RG 59, GRDS, CFPF 1967-69, Box 264, Folder PS 7-1.

284. Telegram from US Mission Berlin to DS, 2 May 1968, NA RG 59, GRDS, CFPF 1967-69, Box 264, Folder PS 7-1.

285. Telegram from US Mission Berlin to DS, 2 May 1968, NA RG 59, GRDS, CFPF 1967-69, Box 264, Folder PS 7-1.

286. Telegram from US Mission Berlin to DS, 3 May 1968, NA RG 59, GRDS, CFPF 1967-69, Box 264, Folder PS 7-1.

287. Telegram from US Mission Berlin to DS, 3 May 1968, NA RG 59, GRDS, CFPF 1967-69, Box 264, Folder PS 7-1.

288. Telegram from US Mission Berlin to DS, 3 May 1968, NA RG 59, GRDS, CFPF 1967-69, Box 264, Folder PS 7-1.

289. Telegram from US Mission Berlin to DS, 3 May 1968, NA RG 59, GRDS, CFPF 1967-69, Box 264, Folder PS 7-1.

290. Telegram from US Mission Berlin to DS, 4 May 1968, NA RG 59, GRDS, CFPF 1967-69, Box 264, Folder PS 7-1.

291. Telegram from US Mission Berlin to DS, 9 May 1968, NA RG 59, GRDS, CFPF 1967-69, Box 264, Folder PS 7-1.

292. Telegram from DS to US Mission Berlin, 8 May 1968, NA RG 59, GRDS, CFPF 1967-69, Box 264, Folder PS 7-1.

293. Telegram from US Mission Berlin to DS, 9 May 1968, NA RG 59, GRDS, CFPF 1967-69, Box 264, Folder PS 7-1.

294. Gerhard Beil, together with a delegation from the GDR's ministry of foreign trade members, traveled to the US from 15 November until 2 December 1972 for private talks with American businessmen and bankers. They were, however, banned from meeting with any US government officials. DS Memorandum, 8 November 1972, NA RG 59 GRDS, RREG 1952-1972, Box 8, Folder V 1.4 Beil, Gerhardt 1972.

295. Telegram from US Mission Berlin to DS, 14 May 1968, NA RG 59, GRDS, CFPF 1967-69, Box 264, Folder PS 7-1.

296. Telegram from DS to US Mission Berlin, 16 May 1968, NA RG 59, GRDS, CFPF 1967-69, Box 264, Folder PS 7-1.

297. Telegram from DS to US Mission Berlin and US Embassy Bonn, 17 May 1968, NA RG 59, GRDS, CFPF 1967-69, Box 264, Folder PS 7-1.

298. Telegram from DS to US Mission Berlin and US Embassy Bonn, 17 May 1968, NA RG 59, GRDS, CFPF 1967-69, Box 264, Folder PS 7-1.

299. Telegram from US Mission Berlin to DS, 20 May 1968, NA RG 59, GRDS, CFPF 1967-69, Box 264, Folder PS 7-1.

300. Telegram from US Mission Berlin to DS, 27 May 1968, NA RG 59, GRDS, CFPF 1967-69, Box 264, Folder PS 7-1.

301. Telegram from US Mission Berlin to DS, 6 June 1968, NA RG 59, GRDS, CFPF 1967-69, Box 264, Folder PS 7-1.

302. Telegram from US Mission Berlin to DS, 6 June 1968, NA RG 59, GRDS, CFPF 1967-69, Box 264, Folder PS 7-1.

303. "Western Allies Denounce East German Travel Curb," *New York Times* (New York, NY), 13 June 1968.

304. "Western Allies Denounce East German Travel Curb," *New York Times* (New York, NY), 13 June 1968.

305. Gehrig, Sebastian. "Cold War Identities: Citizenship, Constitutional Reform, and International Law between East and West Germany,

1967-75." *Journal of Contemporary History* 49, no. 4 (2014): 796, 814. http://www.jstor.org/stable/43697338. (Accessed 29 September 2020).

306. Gehrig, Sebastian. "Cold War Identities: Citizenship, Constitutional Reform, and International Law between East and West Germany, 1967-75."

307. Transcript of tape recording from Ron Wiedenhoeft's interview for Look Magazine, September 1968, property of author.

308. Transcript of tape recording from Ron Wiedenhoeft's interview for Look Magazine, September 1968, property of author.

309. Mary Hellen Battle, *Every Wall Shall Fall* (Old Tappen, NJ: Hewitt House, 1969), p. 299.

310. Lisa Randle, "When Nixon Visited Berlin," Yoshika Loftin Lowe, and Trisha A. Lindsey, *Cold War Memories: A Retrospective on Living in Berlin* (Brats Overseas Books, 2014), p. 203.

311. Transcript of tape recording from Ron Wiedenhoeft's interview for Look Magazine, September 1968, property of author.

312. "Preceptor Recalls Imprisonment," *Columbia Daily Spectator* (New York, NY), 30 October 1968.

313. Bruce Logan's oral history interview with Maxwell Rabb, 19 February 1996, cassette tape 1, property of author.

314. Nicol C. Rae, *The Decline and the Fall of the Liberal Republicans from 1952 to the Present* (New York: Oxford University Press, 1989), 4.

315. Social Security Administration. Social Security History. https://www.ssa.gov/history/ssa/lbjexternal5.html.

316. US Congress, Congressional Record - House. House of Representatives (18 April 1988), 7088 - 7091, http://www.govinfo.gov.

317. Advisory Panel on South Asian Relief Assistance, in Weekly Compilation of Presidential Documents, (Washington, DC: NARA, 1972), 1493-1494.

318. "New Yorker is Reported Choice for Envoy in Italy," *New York Times* (New York, NY), 22 March 1981.

319. US Congress, Congressional Record — House. House of Representatives (18 April 1988), 7089, http://www.govinfo.gov.

320. US Congress, Congressional Record — House. House of Representatives (18 April 1988), 7090, http://www.govinfo.gov.

321. Laura Matysek Wood, "The Hallstein Doctrine: Its Effect as a Sanction," (Master of Arts Thesis, University of North Texas, 1989), p. 2.

322. Gieseke, Jens. *The History of the Stasi — East Germany's Secret Police, 1945-1990*, (New York, NY: Berghahn, 2014), p. 135.

323. Livingston, Robert Gerald, "America's Relationship with the GDR," *Bulletin of the German Historical Institute* 9 (2014): 40-41.

Acknowledgements

This book was a labor of love. As a one-year-old, my father had suddenly and mysteriously vanished from my life, only to reappear as a stranger nine months later. That harrowing experience left lasting scars, casting a long shadow over our family. Many years later, after witnessing the fall of the Berlin Wall and reading his Stasi file, my father was finally able to confront these old demons and acknowledge that his story was worth telling. I am eternally grateful that I had the chance to discuss these experiences openly with him before it was too late.

A very special thanks goes to my mother, Renate Wiedenhoeft, who encouraged and guided my every step. Her recollections as a native Berliner were invaluable. She is the best affirmer, advisor, and reviewer I could have wished for.

Many thanks go to Bernd Feuerherd for his drawing and engineering skills in helping me create map drawings for this book.

A very special thank you goes to the Rabb family for their unwavering support for this project, their kindness and willingness to assist in so many ways. Maxwell Rabb's generosity lives on in his children.

While I was not able to meet all seven prisoners mentioned in this book, my personal meetings with Peter Feinauer and John van Altena made their stories come alive and enriched their narratives immensely.

In the production of this book, I am much indebted to Joe Dugan, Dr. Dieter Dowe, Waltraut Heinze, Günter Meier and Haila Ochs for their insights and wisdom in asking the right questions, offering suggestions, and providing editorial reviews.

My deepest gratitude goes to my husband John for his patience, encouragement, and support, never questioning the value in dedicating so many years of our lives to this project.

Abbreviations

BStU = Zentralarchiv der Bundesbeauftragte für die Unterlagen des Staatssicherheitsdienstes der ehemaligen Deutschen Demokratischen Republik

NA = National Archives at College Park, MD

RG = Record Group

DS = US Department of State

GRDS = General Records of the Department of State

CFPF = Central Foreign Policy Files

CCSF = Classified Central Subject Files

RFSP = Records of the Foreign Service Posts of the Department of State

ETPA = Economic Trade Promotion & Assistance

RRBEA = Records Relating to Berlin & Eastern Affairs

OFCEA = Office of Central European Affairs

RREG = Records Relating to East Germany

Bibliography

Balbier, Uta A., and Christiane Rösch, ed. *Umworbener Klassenfeind — Das Verhältnis der DDR zu den USA*. Berlin: Christoph Links Verlag, 2006.

Battle, Hellen Battle. *Every Wall Shall Fall*. Old Tappan, NJ: Hewitt House, 1969.

Beil, Gerhard. *Außenhandel und Politik - Ein Minister erinnert sich,* Berlin: Edition Ost, Verlag Das Neue Berlin, 2010.

Carter, Miranda. *Anthony Blunt — His Lives*. New York: Picador, 2003.

Erler, Peter, and Hubertus Knabe. *Der verbotene Stadtteil — Stasi-Sperrbezirk Berlin-Hohenschönhausen*. Berlin: Jaron Verlag, 2005.

Fritsche, Susanne. *Die Mauer is gefallen — eine kleine Geschichte der DDR*. München: Carl Hanser Verlag, 2005.

Funder, Anna. *Stasiland: True Stories from behind the Berlin Wall*. London: Granta Publications, 2003.

Gast, Gabriele. *Kundschafterin des Friedens — 17 Jahre Topspionin der DDR beim BND*. Frankfurt, Aufbau Taschenbuch Verlag, 2000.

Gehrig, Sebastian. "Cold War Identities: Citizenship, Constitutional Reform, and International Law between East and West Germany, 1967-75." *Journal of Contemporary History* 49, no. 4, 2014.

Gieseke, Jens. *Der Mielke-Konzern: Die Geschichte der Stasi 1945-1990*. München: Deutsche Verlags-Anstalt, 2001.

Gieseke, Jens. *The History of the Stasi*. New York: Berghahn Books, 2014.

Gizenstat, Stuart. *Imperfect Justice: Looted Assets, Slave Labor, and the Unfinished Business of World War II*. New York: Hachette Book Group, 2009.

Herrin, Moses Reese. "My Conflict with East German Reds." *Ebony Magazine,* June 1967, p. 94-103.

Knabe, Hubertus, ed. *Gefangen in Hohenschönhausen: Stasi-Häftlinge berichten.* Berlin: Ullstein Buchverlage, 2007.

Koehler, John O. *Stasi: The Untold Story of the East German Secret Police.* Boulder, CO: Westview Press, 1999.

McAdams, A. James. *German Divided: From the Wall to Reunification.* Princeton: Princeton University Press, 1993.

Mitchell, Greg. *The Tunnels: Escapes Under the Berlin Wall and the Historic Films the JFK White House Tried to Kill.* New York: Crown Publishing Group, 2016.

Münkel, Daniela, ed. *State Security — A Reader on the GDR Secret Police,* trans. Miriamne Fields. Berlin: Bundesbeauftragte für die Unterlagen des Staatssicherheitsdienstes der ehemaligen Deutschen Demokratischen Republik, 2015.

Murphy, David E., Sergei A. Kondrashew, and George Bailey. *Battle Ground Berlin: CIA vs KGB in the Cold War.* New Haven, CT: Yale University Press, 1997.

Pötzl, Norbert F. *Mission Freiheit Wolfgang Vogel — Anwalt der deutsch-deutschen Geschichte.* Munich: Wilhelm Heyne Verlag, 2014.

Rae, Nicol C. *The Decline and the Fall of the Liberal Republicans from 1952 to the Present.* New York: Oxford University Press, 1989.

Schalck-Golodkowski, Alexander. *Deutsch-deutsche Erinnerungen,* Hamburg: Rowohlt Taschenbuch Verlag, 2001.

Schreiber, Jürgen. *Die Stasi Lebt: Berichte aus einem Unterwanderten Land.* München: Knaur, 2009.

Spiekermann, Uwe, ed. "The Stasi at Home and Abroad: Domestic Order and Foreign Intelligence," *Bulletin of the German Historical Institute* 52, Supplement 9. Washington: German Historical Institute, 2014.

Sturdevant, Christopher. *Cold War Wisconsin.* Charleston, SC: The History Press, 2018.

Van Altena Jr, John. *A Guest of the State.* Chicago: Henry Regnery Company, 1967.

Wiedenhoeft, Ronald. *Berlin's Housing Revolution — German Reform in the 1920s.* Ann Arbor, MI: UMI Research Press, 1971.

Wölben, Jan Philipp. "Der Häftlingsfreikauf aus der DDR 1962/63 - 1989: Zwischen Menschenhandel und humanitären Aktionen," *Wissenschaftliche Reihe des Bundesbeauftragten für die Unterlagen des Staatssicherheitsdienstes der ehemaligen Deutschen Demokratischen Republik,* Analysen und Dokumente, Band 38. Göttingen: Vandenhoeck & Ruprecht, 2014.

Wood, Laura Matysek. "The Hallstein Doctrine: Its Effect as a Sanction". Master of Arts Thesis, University of North Texas, 1989.

Zasimeczuk, Ivan A. "Maxwell M. Rabb: A Hidden Hand of the Eisenhower Administration in Civil Rights and Race Relations." Master of Arts Thesis, Kansas State University, 2008.

9 798987 589397